CHARLES WALDO HASKINS

AN AMERICAN PIONEER IN ACCOUNTANCY

British Library Cataloguing-in-Publication Data
A catalogue record for this book is available from the
British Library

William George Jordan

William George Jordan was born on 6 March 1864 in New York City, USA. He took his university education at the *City College of New York* and began his literary career as an editor of *Book Chat* in 1884. After a brief spell (1888-91) editing *Current Literature* - a magazine offering an eclectic combination of literature review and contemporary commentary, Jordan relocated to Chicago. It was here that he first lectured on his system of Mental Training; although not with any great success. In 1897 Jordan moved back to New York and was hired as the managing editor for *The Ladies Home Journal,* after which he moved on to edit *The Saturday Evening Post.* This substantial editing career is not Jordan's best known achievement however – his essays and thoughts on education and 'mental training' have garnered the most attention. In July 1891 *The Chicago Inter-Ocean* printed an interview with Jordan on his 'mental training'. After the article was published he received so many inquiries that he scheduled a long lecture tour on the subject. *The Inter-Ocean* reported that 'during the past few weeks the calls from Chicago have been so numerous, enthusiastic and positive for lecture courses and private society classes that he has concluded to resign his position in New York and come to Chicago.' In 1894, Jordan published a short pamphlet; *Mental Training, A Remedy for Education,* which opened with the following lines; 'here are two great things that education should do for the individual—it should train his senses, and teach him to think. Education, as we know it to-day, does not truly do either; it gives the individual only a vast accumulation of facts, unclassified, undigested, and seen in no true relations. Like seeds kept in a box, they may be retained, but they do not grow.' Jordan's allegorical style was widely utilised in all his works, and he penned his first book, *The Kingship of Self-Control,* in 1898. This was followed by a further nine texts, all on the subject of self-improvement; a theme which he continued writing on for the rest of his life. *The Majesty of Calmness* (1900) was perhaps his most popular self-help book. Despite these successes, Jordan's most influential writing was actually a political tract. In *The House of Governors* (1907), he aimed to 'promote uniform legislation on vital questions, to conserve states' rights, to lessen centralisation, to secure a fuller, freer voice of the people and to make a stronger nation.' The work was circulated to each state governor and to President Theodore Roosevelt, and was incredibly well received. His ideas were put into practice and the first 'meeting of the governors' was held in Washington, on 18 January, 1910 – with Jordan as its secretary. He was dropped as secretary a year later, but nevertheless, this group is a key part of his legacy.

At the age of fifty-eight, Jordan married Nellie Blanche Mitchell, in New York City at the Grace Episcopal Church. The marriage was a happy one, for the short time it lasted, but sadly Jordan died just six years later of pneumonia on 20 April 1928, at his home in New York.

FOREWORD

IT is fitting that the contribution of Charles Waldo Haskins to the cause of accountancy should be commemorated by the tablet with which the students of the New York University School of Commerce, Accounts, and Finance have honored him.

Mr. Haskins' pride in the profession of accountancy and his labors in raising its standards by means of education had no bounds. The profession of accountancy owes him an everlasting debt of gratitude for the part which he had in shaping its future.

There is much that I might add to the commentary on Mr. Haskins' career but words fail me even as they fail me in giving expression to my love and admiration for him as a friend and partner in professional practice, and to my respect for him as a man.

During my association with him there was no written agreement binding us together in legal relation. That there might be danger of business and professional differences appeared never to have entered his mind. And his attitude in this respect was typical of his magnanimity. He was a profound thinker and scholar: precise in his professional ideals, big in character as well as in stature, and warmly sympathetic in his contact with the world.

The accompanying sketch, written at my request by

Mr. William George Jordan, contains some of the leading incidents of his professional career during our association.

My thanks are due to the Honorable Myron T. Herrick, Mr. Frank A. Vanderlip, Doctor John H. MacCracken, Dean Joseph French Johnson, Professor Leon Brummer, and Mr. H. M. James, all of whom made addresses at the unveiling, and who have kindly given their consent to the publication of these addresses.

ELIJAH W. SELLS.

NEW YORK, February 28, 1922.

TABLE OF CONTENTS

PART I

PART II

SPEAKERS

MYRON T. HERRICK, *Ex-Governor of Ohio*

JOHN H. MACCRACKEN, PH.D.

FRANK A. VANDERLIP, LL.D.

LEON BRUMMER, C.P.A.

H. M. JAMES, B.C.S.

JOSEPH FRENCH JOHNSON, D.C.S., LL.D.

PART I

BIOGRAPHICAL SKETCH

CHARLES WALDO HASKINS

An American Pioneer in Accountancy

I

MORE than three long centuries ago Francis Bacon wrote, in the quaint and rather pompous language of the time: "I hold every man a debtor to his profession; from the which as men of course do seek to receive countenance and profit, so ought they of duty to endeavor themselves by way of amends to be a help and ornament thereto." This means in our every-day English that the individual should be inspired, in his relation to his profession, to give it love, loyalty, and joyous service.

He should think more of his profession than of mere individual profit, as a true soldier holds the "honor of the regiment" ever higher than any mere personal recognition. He should not only be zealous in his care to do naught, as an individual, that would tend to lessen the dignity and fine repute of his profession in the eyes of the world, but he should be ever eager to do all within his power to advance its progress, to add to its popular appreciation, and to increase its prestige.

This was the spirit that inspired the life-work of Charles Waldo Haskins in relation to accountancy.

He was a leader among the sturdy little band of accountants in America who did loyal and devoted service in this cause they loved. He was a pioneer who helped to blaze the way for better things, who awakened others to interest and activity, who organized forces of co-operation, and who did his big part in clearing the ground and seeding it for the great harvests that have come from it. No true history of accountancy can ever be written that does not recognize the vital part in its development played by Mr. Haskins with others in laying the foundation of a profession destined to a still higher and greater future.

The beginnings of important movements and institutions, the human interest details, are so often lost because they are not set down at a time when the facts are still in the memory of men yet living, that it seems fitting to put on record this slight study of accountancy in America, together with what Charles Waldo Haskins contributed to its progress. As 1922 marks the seventieth anniversary of his birth, this sketch of his life and activities may serve as a memorial to his years of unselfish consecration and of valued service to his profession.

He was born January 11, 1852, in the Borough of Brooklyn, New York, of a long line of American ancestors, sterling, aggressive fighters for freedom in time of war and for ideas and progress in time of peace. His ancestry is worth noting here in detail for the double reason that it reveals the sturdy mental and moral qualities persisting in a nineteenth century life that made Mr. Haskins what he was, and because it throws a strong sidelight on his interest, initiative, and inspiration in founding and perpetuating many of our best-known patriotic societies.

The first of the Haskins to come to America was Robert, who went to Boston either direct from England or by way of the Province of Virginia, and we may accept either the one or the other of the conflicting accounts. We know, however, that in 1728 he married Sarah, daughter of Philip Cook of Cambridge.

In the second generation, John, the son of Robert and Sarah, became a prominent figure in the life of Boston. When only eighteen, at the outbreak of hostilities between France and England for control of the growing and thriving territories, thrilled with patriotic fervor, he entered the service as a privateer aboard a letter-of-marque vessel bound for the West Indies and was in turn taken prisoner by both Spain and France. He read the handwriting on the wall, of the struggle that must come between England and the colonies and prepared himself for the conflict. When the alarm was sounded at Lexington, as captain of a Boston company he distinguished himself and was later a powerful figure in the conferences and fights of such a group as that of the Adams family, Joseph Warren, Josiah Quincy, and other patriots who have left brilliant names in our Revolutionary history. His wife, Hannah Upham, was sister to the Reverend Henry Dunster, first president of Harvard College, and was descended from John Howland, one of the forty-one pilgrims who signed the constitution of government of the new colony as it lay on the lid of Elder Brewster's chest in the dimly-lighted and crowded cabin of the Mayflower.

In the third generation was Robert Haskins, son of "Honest John" Haskins, the patriot named above, and great-grandfather of Charles Waldo Haskins. He was a prominent and successful merchant of Boston. His wife, Rebecca, was daughter of the Reverend William Emerson, who built the "Old Manse" in Concord, Mass., where, about seventy years later, Hawthorne wrote his great books. Rebecca Haskins was the aunt of Ralph Waldo Emerson and was descended from a long line of eminent divines and scholars.

Thomas Waldo Haskins, son of Robert and Rebecca and grandfather of our Mr. Haskins, was born in Boston in 1801, and early entered the mercantile life, becoming the largest dealer in hardware in his native city and one of its most prominent citizens.

The early years of the nineteenth century were years of special stress and storm in New England. Foreign trade was at a low ebb, factories were running on part time, money was scarce, and everyone felt the strain. Many of the younger generation sought fresher and more fruitful fields of hope and enterprise, and among them was Waldo Emerson Haskins, son of Thomas and his wife, Mary Soren, who at the age of twenty-four came to New York and entered the banking house of his uncle, George Soren. Shortly after, he married Amelia Rowan Cammeyer, daughter of Charles Cammeyer, and the young couple moved to Brooklyn. It was here that Charles Waldo Haskins was born.

II

The "City of Churches," as it was called, was then a town of less than a hundred thousand people, and it had not yet begun to absorb neighboring villages as it did later, to be in turn swallowed up by the big city across the river. The public school system was still rather primitive, and young Haskins received his early training in private schools of the city. His parents had decided for him that he was to become a civil engineer, and when ready he entered the Polytechnic Institute of Brooklyn, from which he was graduated at the early age of fifteen.

Young as he was at this time, he showed so strongly the dawn of the powers that later made him eminent in his profession, that Dr. David H. Cochran, president of the Institute, an able educator and a keen student of human nature, predicted for the boy a brilliant future. After his graduation, he began to think for himself as to his life-work, and the thought of civil engineering as a career grew less and less alluring the longer he considered it. He had made a splendid record in mathematics and he loved "figuring" in all its phases; consequently he turned his attention to accounting.

He secured a position in the accounting department of the old and highly reputed importing house of

Frederick Butterfield & Co. of New York City. Here he remained for five years, adding practical experience to his theoretical knowledge; he learned the vital part that figures play in business; he began to see in a vague way that they represented something higher and more important than mere bookkeeping, and that, properly marshaled and mobilized in orderly array from a clearly preconceived angle, they would throw a new illumination on business plans, policies, and progress.

After his five years apprenticeship to this valuable training, he wanted to go abroad where he could think it all over in new surroundings, see business and life through a different atmosphere, and determine for himself what he wanted to do and how he would do it. He spent two years in Paris in the study of art, for which he had both taste and talent, and made a tour of Europe, finding accountancy much further developed on the Continent than in America. This time abroad was invaluable to him. His keen, observing mind gathered much upon which he thought deeply; he learned to depend on himself, to respect his own judgment, and to abide by his own decisions. The trip gave him, too, that ease and poise in meeting men that was so marked a characteristic in his later years and which proved so vital a factor in his success.

Upon his return to New York, he entered Wall Street, forming a temporary connection with the banking and brokerage firm of his father. This was another influence slowly shaping him for his real career. While he was engaged with Butterfield & Co., he saw the relationship of accountancy to foreign trade and all its multiform phases and problems. In Wall Street the figures were connected with finance and the rise and fall of stocks, and he was soon to see the spell that figures exercised in relation to railroad construction and transportation activities, mammoth organizations and business enterprises, with their infinite multiplicity of details, all finally expressed in a series of figures.

III

At this time accountancy in America was a poor, weak, struggling thing, with its possibilities unrecognized even by those within its ranks. It was not a profession; it was but a business adjunct, and not much of one at that. The accountant was little more than a bookkeeper and the line of demarcation between the two was slight indeed. Accountancy had no ideals, no organization, no inspiration and influence. It required a man of big vision to see what it might become; to see in the weak elements of its present the glorious possibilities of its final evolution into a liberal profession—respected, honored, and recognized in its dignity and usefulness in the eyes of men.

Mr. Haskins had this vision. With the imagination of a poet and the intuition of a prophet, he realized what accountancy could become, and he determined to do his part toward vitalizing it to the fulfillment of its destiny. He conceived of accountancy in this country advancing to the same degree of perfection common in Europe, and then outstripping and surpassing the profession on the Continent in great strides when the business world of America should waken, American industry realize the need of the new profession, and American finance welcome and depend on accountancy for its own finer development.

Mr. Haskins felt all this, and felt it deeply. His study and observation in Europe had given him a glimpse of the higher possibilities of accountancy and it became the great, serious purpose of his life to establish new ideals in the American field and to help realize them. He gave up his Wall Street connections and entered the accounting department of the North River Construction Company, which was then building the New York, West Shore and Buffalo Railroad. So marked was his success here, that he soon had entire supervision of all the construction accounts of the company. When the West Shore was completed, he was retained in the service of the railroad as general bookkeeper and auditor of disbursements until the road was absorbed by the New York Central.

A red-letter day in his life was that day in 1886 when he opened an office of his own in New York City and entered the profession of public accounting on his own responsibility. Aside from his regular duties, he held in the several years following, numerous important executive positions. Thus we find him serving with distinction as secretary of the Manhattan Trust Company and of the Old Dominion Construction Company, comptroller of the Central of Georgia Railway, comptroller of the Ocean Steamship Company, comptroller of the Chesapeak and Western Railroad, and receiver of the Augusta Mining and Investment Company.

Each of these additional responsibilities was a new opportunity; a new privilege of service. He was coming face to face with new problems and new solutions of the old ones; business and financial activities were being remodeled along broader lines; consolidations, reorganizations, the formation of trusts and other big aggregations demanded new and better methods of accounting.

IV

Two rivers, rising far apart, one flowing from the east and the other from the west, may meet and unite their waters and ever after move as a single mighty stream toward the open sea. Something analogous to this sometimes happens in the lives of human beings. Two men of strong individuality and of differing characteristics, each unaware even of the existence of the other, may, by what we call chance, meet, unite in the bonds of friendship, and work together toward the accomplishment of a common purpose—the attainment of the same ideals.

Thus it was in 1893, in the meeting of Charles Waldo Haskins and Elijah Watt Sells in a hotel in Washington. The meeting was the beginning of a fine friendship which was to grow into esteem, confidence, and affection in their later years of partnership, unclouded by a single moment of misunderstanding. It was a spirit of rare romance in business that inspired both men during their years together to a common devotion.

The meeting came about in this way: Within a few years after the adoption of the Constitution of the United States, when the young republic was getting into working shape, the necessity of reform in the business methods of the Executive Departments began to be felt. In the decades following there were three or four efforts at investigation made by Government committees, but they were unavailing, casual, and unproductive of results. There was endless red-tape, divided responsibility, wasted effort, unnecessary delay, and duplication of work.

The condition had grown up through many administrations, in many ways easy to understand but difficult to remedy. In 1892 Secretary Foster of the Treasury Department saw a great light when he stated that "in the nature of things it is impossible for committees of Congress, with other duties and obligations, to give their entire time to a study of this great problem, and the same is true as to a commission composed of officers and clerks in the Treasury Department." He pointed out that even if they could spare the time, trained as they were to existing conditions, it was but natural to suppose that they would be slow to recommend radical changes.

Secretary Foster strongly recommended the appointment of a non-partisan commission, limited in its existence to a period of three years, organized exclusively for the purpose of examining existing methods of business and work in the executive departments, and of making recommendations for newer, better, more economical, and more efficient methods along safer, saner business lines.

V

This seed of suggestion fell into fertile soil in the brain of Alexander M. Dockery, Representative from Missouri. He was a man of keen analytic mind and of hard, practical, common sense. He had been accustomed, when president of a country bank at Gallatin, Mo., to the simplest, readiest, and most methodical ways of doing business. While serving as a member of the Committee on Appropriations in the Fifty-first and Fifty-second Congresses, he was brought into close touch with the chiefs of bureaus in the Departments and knew the red tape and inefficiency that complicated the conduct of their business.

There were methods, he felt convinced, that could be devised by experts, practical men of business who were tried and tested by experience in handling the affairs of corporations, which would simplify the work of the Departments, save the money of the people, expedite the service, and make it more efficient. He realized, however, that the time was not ripe and he waited. In 1892, on the election of Grover Cleveland to a second term, with the Cabinet, the Senate, and the House Democratic, and the administration pledged to economy and retrenchment, he felt he could handle the opposition that would come from the army of employes in constant fear less the jobs of many of them be endangered.

Toward the end of the short term of the Fifty-second Congress, he secured an order from the House giving the Committee on Appropriations the power of attaching to their appropriation bill the creation of a Joint Commission of three members of the House and three of the Senate of the Fifty-third Congress. The duties of the Commission were to investigate the status of laws organizing the Executive Departments, to examine into the operation of employes and methods and to make recommendations to improve the service.

The Commission was created by an act of Congress approved March 3, 1893, as follows:

"That a Joint Commission, consisting of three Senators, members of the Fifty-third Congress, to be appointed by the present President of the Senate, and three members-elect to the House of Representatives of the Fifty-third Congress, to be appointed by the Speaker of the House of Representatives of the Fifty-second Congress shall, during the Fifty-third Congress, inquire into and examine the status of the laws organizing the Executive Departments, bureaus, divisions, and other Government establishments at the national capital; the rules, regulations, and methods for the conduct of the same; the time and attention devoted to the operations thereof by the persons employed therein, and the degree of efficiency of all such employes; whether any modification of these laws can be made to secure greater efficiency and economy; and whether a reduction in the number or compensation of the persons authorized to be employed in said Executive Departments, or bureaus, can be made without injury to the public service: Provided,

"That the Commission herein authorized shall have no jurisdiction to inquire into and report on pension legislation. Said Commission is authorized to employ not exceeding three experts who shall render such assistance as the Commission may require in the prosecution of the investigation herein required and shall receive such compensation as the Commission shall determine to be just and reasonable. The heads of the respective Executive Departments shall detail from time to time such officers and employes as may be requested by said Commission in their investigations. Said Commission or any subcommittee thereof shall have power to send for persons and papers, and to administer oaths, and such process shall be issued, and such oaths administered by the Chairman of the Commission or sub-committee and the Commission may report by bill or otherwise to their respective Houses of the Fifty-third Congress. All necessary expenses of said Commission shall be paid out of any money in the Treasury not otherwise appropriated, upon vouchers approved jointly by the Chairman of said Commission."

This Commission would probably have accomplished as little as countless other committees of investigation, were it not for the insertion in the act of a big, practical, new idea. It occupied but half a dozen lines but it meant everything for the success of the work. It ran thus: "Said Commission is authorized to employ

not exceeding three experts, who shall render such
assistance as the Commission may require in the
prosecution of the investigation herein required, and
shall receive such compensation as the Commission
shall determine to be just and reasonable."

The personnel of the Commission, which soon became popularly known as the "Dockery Commission,"
was composed of Mr. A. M. Dockery, who was elected
Chairman, James D. Richardson of Tennessee, Nelson
Dingley, Jr., of Maine, F. M. Cockrell of Missouri,
James K. Jones of Arkansas, and Shelby M. Cullom
of Illinois. The first three members represented the
Senate; the last three the House. The first work of
the Commission was to find the experts who could
carry through successfully this colossal task and the
search for these experts occupied from six weeks to
two months.

The men finally selected were Mr. Joseph W. Reinhardt, Mr. Charles Waldo Haskins, and Mr. Elijah
Watt Sells. Mr. Reinhardt had, only a few years
before, been head of the accounting department of
the Atchison, Topeka, and Santa Fe Railroad. A
plan which he had made for the reorganization of the
road, secured for him the position of its president.
Business disturbances in 1893, from which the Company suffered, were the cause of its bankruptcy. He
did no detail work in connection with the Dockery
Commission and resigned shortly, leaving the whole
campaign to his two associates.

Mr. Sells came from the West, where he had a wide
experience in the line of work he was now to under-

take. He began his career in accounting as a railway station agent. Because of his success and accuracy in handling figures there, he was transferred to the general office and engaged from time to time upon freight accounts, ticket accounts, car mileage accounts, and similar work. He also held various positions in the accounting department, such as general bookkeeper, chief clerk in the comptroller's office, assistant comptroller, paymaster, auditor, secretary, and vice-president. Besides, he had frequently engaged in reviewing accounts of other operations incidental to railways, such as those of coal companies, steamship companies, sawmill and lumber companies, hotel companies and others, with some engagements to make reports upon corporations quite apart from railway interests. His last position with a railroad was for the express purpose of making such reports. Much of this work was in later years akin to public accounting practice. From this position he was granted a leave of absence to engage on the work of the Dockery Commission with Mr. Haskins.

VI

The first meeting of these two men who were to carry through together a great undertaking was in Washington, when Mr. Sells on reaching that city called on Mr. Haskins at his hotel. The Chinese say that a child is one year old at its birth; there are friendships that seem already to have age at the very beginning, and in the first quarter of an hour two men may come closer together in sympathetic understanding and harmony of ideals and purpose than others could in decades. So it was with Mr. Haskins and Mr. Sells.

The two men sat down at their first breakfast together, a meal that was a golden memory to each of them in their years of later association as friends and partners. They spoke, in a general way, of the important work upon which they were entering but this was merely incidental; the planning and details were matters of the days to come when they were actually face to face with the problems. They talked in a personal, revealing way, with the ease and confidence of fine comradeship, and found a unity in their attitude toward life and in their ideals and purposes that gave a solid foundation for their future association.

It was fortunate for them and for the work upon which they were engaged that this was so. During the two years upon which they were now entering, had the two men not been in perfect accord, there would have been countless occasions where differences of opinions as to plan, policy, or methods, and pettiness or jealousies would have lessened their efficiency and diminished greatly the success of their work. But there was no lack of harmony; no break in their mutual understanding. Differing in many ways in type and characteristics, the qualities of the one supplemented those of the other, and together they worked as one man. On June 12, 1893, they entered upon their labors in a room set apart for them in the Treasury Department, with the hearty support and cordial co-operation of President Cleveland and all the members of the Cabinet.

Oliver Wendell Holmes has the line in one of his poems: "I did not dare to be as funny as I could." The two experts had gone but a little way in their investigations before they found that they did not dare to be as sweeping and radical in their recommendations as they longed to be. They wanted to secure the maximum of results in the way of better methods in accounting and in efficiency, yet they realized that if they sought to accomplish too much they might imperil all. On the one hand they had to deal with the Commission, men busy with manifold other duties and interests; on the other hand, with the employes in the various Departments who felt their positions insecure and who consequently grew increasingly anxious and worried as the days went on.

The work of the experts required not only rare accounting ability and business knowledge and experience in relation to the conduct of great corporations—for they were investigating the accounting system of the United States Government, the greatest business corporation in the world—but also keen analysis, clear judgment, and infinite tact and wisdom in the handling of men and measures.

VII

In the beginning, the work of the Joint Commission was not taken very seriously, even in Congress, the general attitude being one of indifference and of smiling tolerance—tolerance such as that with which one might regard Don Quixote trying to stop the gigantic sails of the wind-mills. Investigations had been many. They had come and gone with no harvest of results, usually expensive but nevertheless harmless, started to please some one in power or to placate an aroused public which went to sleep again, or was diverted by some new interest before the investigation was complete. One of the Senators expressed the general view pretty fairly when he said: "Oh, it's all right; it amuses Dockery and doesn't do any harm."

But this was only in the beginning. The atmosphere soon changed. It was but a short time before the Joint Commission proved itself a real force. It was actually doing things as it listened to the reports and recommendations of the experts who were quietly plugging along with their figures, examinations, and conferences, undisturbed by the growing storm of opposition they were creating. The recommendations of the experts were so clear, final, and self evident in their business common-sense that one bill after another reported by the Commission to Congress went through, or became in force by regulations or orders.

The press of the country was, in general, in hearty accord with the aims and purposes of the Commission and with the practical, sound, business methods of Mr. Haskins and Mr. Sells. The newspapers recognized the investigation as a sincere, earnest, non-partisan effort to bring about better conditions in the administration of the affairs of the country, and they watched with interest every step in the progress of the work. They saw it all impersonally, calmly, and in relation to the welfare of the whole country.

The papers of Washington, nearer the fighting line, were in a different atmosphere. The personal equation here counted as a factor. It affected the interests of a large class of their readers—employes in the Departments whose positions might be imperiled by some stroke of the ax of reform, wielded by the Commission and made by the two experts who were doing so much to disturb the established order of things. Editorials became frequent on the danger of retrenchment, the wrong of depriving clerks of their positions, and similar topics. Letters appeared, too, in the papers from "Clericus," "An Old Clerk," "Pro Bono Publico," "Old Subscriber," and others who could not see or would not see that mere retrenchment was not the aim of the Commission, but better and more efficient and effective service.

Mr. Haskins put the whole situation concisely when he was asked one day if the Commission was working to cut down the expenses of the Departments. "That

is only an incident," he said. "The Commission is trying to simplify work so that it can be done more rapidly
and more effectively. With simpler methods it can be
done by fewer clerks, in some offices. But what we
want to do is to place the Departments in position to
do current work. If you take a claim for back pay or
bounty to a Department now, they put it in a pigeon-
hole—in what they call their open files—and there it
lies for two years before it is even taken up for consideration. The business is simply congested. With
a different system there is no reason why the work
should not be brought up to date."

But Government clerks, holding their pay envelopes
so close to their eyes as to eclipse the sun, could not be
expected to understand or appreciate. For this they
were not to be blamed. It was natural for them to be
afraid of losing their positions and to be anxious about
those dependent on them. So strong was this anxiety,
that boisterous opposition arose from an ex-employe
of the Treasury who had become an attorney for an
association of clerks.

This man's strongest argument in objecting to the
work of the Commission was that it was presumptuous
for Congress to venture to improve on the work of
Alexander Hamilton. There was a child-like ignor-
ance in his mind of the fact that the system of accounting in use in the Treasury had changed and become
highly complicated since the time of Hamilton, and
that, even if it were identical, the law-making body of
the United States was in a better position to meet
present-day requirements and problems than some one
living under different conditions a century ago.

VIII

The attitude of the employes of the Government toward the Dockery Commission was cleverly and humorously set forth in a poem entitled "Mr. Dockery's Commission," published "with apologies to James Whitcomb Riley," in one of the Washington papers. The verses were very popular; they were cut out and carried in pocket-books till they were worn thin at the creases, and were passed from hand to hand. They read as follows:

"The Department Joint Commission's come to our place to stay,
To stir the chiefs an' clerks up an' shoo the drones away,
An' examine into business an' ask how things are done,
An' see that guv'ment workers give us value for their "mun."
An' all the poor Department clerks, when daily tasks are through,
Sit 'round their lowly firesides when the wind goes "Woo-oo!"
A-listenin' to the threats 'at all the people tell about,
That Dockery'll git you
    Ef you
      Don't
        Watch
          Out!

"When the children of the household are all snuggled in their
    beds,
An' draw the sheet an' blanket roun' an' kuvver up their heads,
Pa an' Ma still talk it over, what a fearful thing it is,
This Department Joint Commission, with inquiries into biz.
Their dreams are full of frightful things an' awful sights an'
    sounds,
While the demons that beset them there cavort with leaps an'
    bounds

An' from every horrid throat comes forth the terrifyin' shout
That Dockery'll git you
    Ef you
        Don't
           Watch
              Out!

"So this dreffel Joint Commission is a-makin' matters hum,
An' is keepin' the Department clerks right down beneath its
    thumb,
It's makin' life a burden to the wicked an' the good,
Tho' its ultimate intentions can be scarcely understood.
Still it's goin' thro' the bureaus an' a-turnin' things aroun'
An' sez it will reform 'em from the top clean to the ground,
While the clerks all list in terror to the rumors flyin' about,
That Dockery'll git you
    Ef you
        Don't
           Watch
              Out!"

The story of what this investigation did and the reforms it accomplished is worth giving in some detail, for many reasons. It was not only a great event in the life of Mr. Haskins and of his associate, Mr. Sells, but it had a large significance in the history of public accounting in America, and was a fine tribute to the value of the service that the profession, represented by these two men, could render to the Government. Large corporations had been availing themselves more and more of the experience and counsel of trained accountants, but this was the first time that the Government of the United States had recognized the profession and called in any of its members to investigate its methods and to suggest improvements in its system of accounting.

It was a concession that the conduct of the affairs

of a great nation such as ours is merely the management of a business on a colossal scale, exactly the same in principle as the management of a railroad or other large corporation. To secure the performance of all these manifold activities and functions of government with the maximum efficiency and effectiveness, in accord with the best principles of business and with the minimum expense of time, money, and energy in every detail, was the secret of sane and sound government.

IX

The work of the experts, therefore, was to suggest methods of simplifying the keeping of accounts: cutting out duplication of effort and record; reducing wasted motion and unnecessary work to its lowest point; eliminating superfluous links in the chain of relation through different offices, as a railroad company seeks constantly to lower its grade and to shorten its track; standardizing dates for certain work where such uniformity counts for efficiency and economy; supplanting divided responsibility by single responsibility vested where it naturally belonged; discontinuing work or offices that had outlived their usefulness; installing new and better methods to expedite the service of Departments so that they would be up-to-date instead of months and years behind; and improving the effectiveness of the conduct of business while lessening the number of employes but not increasing their individual burdens.

Such, in brief, is the general outline of what Mr. Haskins and Mr. Sells sought to accomplish. The measure of their success may be judged by the reforms which, through the action of the Joint Commission, were put into effect by regulations and general orders and, in some instances, through laws passed by Congress.

The first measure reported by the Commission to the House and the Senate was a concurrent resolution adopting printing on parchment instead of engrossing as the process of enrolling future bills. Since the very first Congress, bills had been engrossed on parchment and one copy submitted to the Speaker of the House and one to the President for signature. It was a slow process and was found to lead to many errors in transcription, and this to a larger extent than in printed matter. In the Tariff Act of 1883, for instance, it was intended to place fruitplants on the free list but the clerk in engrossing the bill inadvertently put in a comma between fruit and plants, thus putting all fruits on the list of duty-free articles. This little blunder cost the Government about $2,500,000 a year in lost revenue. The printing plan increased accuracy, lessened the expense, and decreased the time required in transcription.

The sixth auditor's office, a most important bureau of the Treasury Department, the activities of which are devoted to handling the accounts of the Post-Office Department, was found to be over a year behind in its work. There was unnecessary bookkeeping, long delay in settling accounts, bad method, and what one member of the Commission called "an appalling amount of red tape."

It was shown that the money-order business had not increased during the preceding ten years despite the rapid growth of the country, and that the express companies were getting the business of orders for the larger amounts while the Post Office Department had been carrying the bulk of its orders for smaller amounts at a loss. New rates were established and a new form of money-order blank invented by the experts, with a "margin-check," safeguarding the public and greatly expediting the checking up of postmasters' money-order accounts.

The postal note, which had proven unsatisfactory because it afforded no security whatever and no legal means of duplication if lost, was abolished. The money-order for amounts under $2.50 at the same rate as the postal note took its place with the assurance of security.

The Government, it was shown, was paying more to postmasters for issuing and paying money-orders than it received itself. This policy was condemned by the Commission as "unbusiness-like and improvident," and was changed by a reduction of the amount paid. And the postmasters found the change more profitable to themselves because of the greater number of money-orders issued under the new system.

A host of other minor changes, all expediting the service, together with a smaller number of clerks, resulted in a saving of about $80,000 a year in this branch of post office activities.

In the case of a number of these reforms, the Postmaster-General did not take kindly to them at first and at one meeting of the Commission and the experts it was necessary to labor zealously with him until one o'clock in the morning. When, however, it was all carefully proved to him, he was thoroughly convinced and did all in his power to put the recommendations through.

In the Treasury Department, it was found that there was much confusion in the laws and regulations governing the returns for property. These returns were made for the purpose of effecting a check as to the receipt and disposition of property and supplies in the custody of the officers and subordinates in the various Executive Departments. A large amount of time, money, and energy was wasted in the auditing of these papers. The experts proved that the work was unnecessary—complicating the system and delaying the returns with coils of red tape. Their recommendations led to the saving of about $15,000 a year in this one detail.

X

One of the most important of the reforms carried through by the Commission was that changing the accounting system of the Treasury Department in the matter of auditing the accounts of customs officers. The bill, in twenty sections, abolished the offices of second comptroller, deputy second comptroller, and deputy first comptroller, and vested the duties and responsibilities of these offices in the hands of the first comptroller. This gave the legal direction in the settlement of accounts to one head and prevented the confusion arising from the existence of two officers with the same powers, making different interpretations. The new method of handling the accounts expedited public business and increased the security of the Government through a more speedy settlement of the accounts of officials, disbursing officers, and others charged with the custody of the public money, by requiring them to make prompt returns under strict provisions. In addition to facilitating this work, the reform had the economical value of reducing the cost by about $200,000 a year.

In the Interior Department, the experts found that contested public land cases had been fomented and increased by the Act of May 14, 1880, which gave priority in entry on any successfully contested claim.

This practically amounted to a bonus to informers, a state of affairs which the experts declared was "an odious system, liable to abuse for purposes of blackmail." In actual experience, it resulted in hardship to innocent and poor settlers through having their claims held up by a contestant and through delay in the Interior Department. And there was always the risk that some technicality would cause their patents finally to be refused, thereby depriving them of their just rights and property. The correction of this evil by amending the Act of 1880 so as to eliminate the offending section, was a good thing in itself and incidentally it lopped off, at one stroke, about $32,000 a year from the expense account of the Interior Department. Other evils relating to the public lands, notably in regard to the engrossing and recording of land patents, were corrected through the efforts of the Commission, acting upon the detailed suggestions of Mr. Haskins and Mr. Sells. The result was a greatly facilitated service and a saving of nearly $24,000 a year.

It had been the practice of each of the Departments to order its own fuel, ice, stationery, and other needed supplies by separate advertisements and contracts. There was no uniformity in prices, no satisfaction in quality, no common standard in judging. One Department would pay 13 cents a hundred for ice while another paid 30 cents; coal for one branch of the Government cost $4.66 a ton, while the price paid by another branch was $5.14 a ton, and similar differences ran through all lines of supplies. The Commission fixed uniform dates for inviting proposals for all Departments and Government offices, under the control of a Board constituted for this purpose to examine all bids. This meant a cutting down in the expense for advertising, a more clearly defined method of passing on quality, and the assurance of the lowest market price through the combined buying power of many orders bunched as one. The example is typical of many of the minor evils the Commission corrected on the suggestion of its experts—evils that would not have been tolerated by any private corporation, yet which persisted in the Government unrecognized and unnoted, simply because the Departments failed to co-operate and because there was no central agency to see them in their inter-relation and to mass their common needs by a uniform policy.

XI

While investigating the methods of the Treasury Department, it was found that the Treasurer of the United States was making an annual report to Congress, under the statute, which was so voluminous and so unintelligible as to be practically useless. It gave the name of every person to whom the Government paid money during the year, together with the amount of the payment. No one in Congress or anywhere else ever looked at it, yet it appeared regularly each year. Its discontinuance saved about $7,000 a year.

In the study of the details of the bonding of officers of the Government, it was shown that there was great confusion in the laws relating to the approval of bonds and the determination of those not fixed by Congress. No provision was made for the periodic examination of the bonds to determine their adequacy or solvency. Many reforms were suggested and carried through in matters of this kind. The discontinuance of personal bonds and the substitution therefor of bonds by companies organized to do business of this character resulted in an annual saving estimated at about $70,000 a year.

It was not the intent of the Commission to investigate any branches of the Government service outside of Washington, but Secretary Carlisle was anxious that the methods in use at the New York Custom House should be reviewed by the experts of the Commission. They accordingly made a thorough examination of conditions and systems there. The result of the investigation showed that the business methods were cumbersome and obselete and required a much larger force than was necessary to carry on the work effectively and efficiently. Modern labor-saving devices and up-to-date systems, in every-day use in the conduct of banking, railroad, and other live business enterprises, were unknown at the Custom House.

The Commission reported that the Custom House had been more of a political machine than a business institution and stated that the most desirable appointments had been parceled out for many years to politicians instead of to business men and technical experts. The recommendations made by the Commission in great detail covered the consolidation of a number of unimportant offices, the reduction of the clerical force, and the introduction of comparatively modern systems of bookkeeping, recording, filing, and conducting correspondence. The Commission, through its experts, made an examination of the Custom Houses of Boston and Philadelphia and found conditions there practically the same as they found them in New York.

XII

These are but a few of the reforms which the Dockery Commission, acting on the investigations and recommendations of Mr. Haskins and Mr. Sells, accomplished in improving the business methods and the accounting system of the Government of the United States. It was a great undertaking, most successfully carried through along safe, practical lines of business administration. The success of the undertaking was attested by the cordial appreciation of the press of the country, the testimony of the heads of the Departments, and the proof of results in more efficient service at a lower cost in the years that followed the completion of the work.

The real need for the work, in all its actuality of detail, was not realized by Congress or the general public in the beginning. The whole situation was put graphically and vividly by Mr. Edward I. Remick, at that time Chief Clerk of the State Department and for many years prior to that employed in the Treasury Department. He was a loyal and able assistant in many ways to Mr. Haskins and Mr. Sells in their investigations, and his advice was frequently sought in the preparation of certain bills incident to their work.

One day Mr. Remick was asked whether or not he favored a change in the accounting system, such as the labors of the experts would bring forth. His answer was straight from the shoulder but was given with the anecdotal turn that was so popular with Lincoln. "There was once in a far Western town," he said, "a man with crossed eyes, a broken nose, and projecting teeth, who held the leather medal of the Ugly Club. He was unable to find a man uglier than himself to whom it could be transferred. One day he was kicked by a mule and as his looks could not be made worse, the accident resulted in really improving them. The accounting system of the Treasury is so ugly in its features that however hard it may be kicked, it cannot but be improved—in fact there is no accounting system. That which was set up in the early days of the republic and was known as the Hamilton system because it was put into operation when he was at the head of the Treasury, is not the system which obtains today, although it is palmed off on the public as such."

XIII

The two years of the investigation of the Government's methods of keeping its accounts and conducting its business ended on March 4, 1895. It was successful from every standpoint; the reforms instituted were safe, sane, and practicable, dictated by clear vision and sound business common sense. It vindicated the view taken by Secretary Foster, that independent, free-minded, outside forces should investigate conditions and methods and suggest reforms, rather than those within the Departments.

The estimated annual saving effected by the Commission at the time it completed its work, through laws or rulings then in operation, was $607,591, and the amount on other reforms proposed by the Commission but not yet acted upon at the time it closed its work was $449,928.

Of the saving effected as the result of the reforms introduced, $360,000 represented salaries, and called for the elimination of 251 clerks. Of this the largest single item was in the Treasury Department, where salaries amounting to $239,000, corresponding to 176 employes, were eliminated.

Notwithstanding the large savings effected and recommended, the expense of the Commission was only $41,264.23. In considering this item, cognizance should be taken of the fact that the total amount recommended for elimination was $1,057,519, and that the work leading up to the recommendations not yet adopted at the time the Commission concluded its efforts, occupied a considerable time covered by the expense. The money-saving, while large, represented only a small part of what the Commission really accomplished.

After stating that the total expenses of the Commission had been only $41,264.23, while the net annual saving amounted to $607,591, the report continues: "This reduction is not made for the time being only, but will continue through each of the coming years. The Commission, however, feels that the expedition of public business and added security to the Government in its methods of accounting under the new systems inaugurated would have fully justified its existence even if there had been no diminution of expenditures."

The figures of the Commission as to savings are ultra-conservative. They are under-estimates as may be shown by two or three typical instances: In the substitution of printing for engrossing in the enrolling of bills, the Commission contented itself by saying, "it will considerably reduce expenses," yet no record of even an estimate of saving on this item is given in the recapitulation. In the report "there is an estimate of the force required in the Land Office for reproducing the press-copy letter books and should the plan recommended by the Commission for doing this work be adopted, it would cost $85,000 less than the amount estimated by the General Land Office." The abolition of the office of Solicitor of Internal Revenue not only saved his salary ($4,500) as stated, but it also removed the expense of the salary of his secretary, which was $1,500 a year. There were many other items of economy that the Commission, for some reason, did not insert in its recapitulations.

XIV

In addition to all the direct results of the work of the Commission, was the big, new moral force it brought into the Departments—the inspiration, initiative, and influence, and the inculcation of a "better way" as a principle among the workers.

From the heads of Departments affected by reforms instituted by the Commission, and from other Government officials came, shortly after the changed conditions became apparent, cordial letters of appreciation and congratulation. The Commission, in all its many recommendations "was unanimous and at no time was its work hampered by personal interests or vexed by partisan controversies."

The Honorable Redfield Proctor of Vermont said in the United States Senate on July 15, 1894: "In regard to the experts who were employed by the Commission, I have seen much of them and have spent a great deal of time with them in going over the details of their recommendations. I have a very high opinion of their ability. I think the Commission was peculiarly fortunate in their selection. I confess my only surprise was that they were so very fortunate. These men are thoroughly competent, experienced, and skillful; and have been extremely careful and conservative in their methods."

The testimonial presented to Mr. Haskins and Mr. Sells, expressive of the appreciation by the Commission of the valued service rendered by the experts is here given in facsimile. Aside from the personal recognition it tenders, this testimonial is an eloquent tribute to accountancy as a whole in its acknowledgment of service to a great Government.

OFFICE OF

The Joint Commission of Congress

TO INQUIRE INTO THE STATUS OF LAWS ORGANIZING
THE EXECUTIVE DEPARTMENTS

Washington D.C. March 2nd, 1895.

Messrs C.W. Haskins and C.M. Sells.
Experts under the Joint Commission, etc.

Gentlemen:

In conducting the work of this Commission, it affords me especial pleasure to express to you my appreciation of the valuable services you have rendered. To your rare business capacity, and peculiar adaptation to analyzing old and formulating plans for new methods, is in great measure due the credit for the reorganization of the accounting system of the United States Government. It was in many respects the most arduous and important undertaking of the kind in the history of the country, and its success in expediting and simplifying the public business without removing any of the necessary safeguards has been fully demonstrated and attested by all of the officials affected thereby.

Very respectfully,

Alex. M. Dockery

Chairman Joint Commission

TESTIMONIAL OF THE JOINT COMMISSION OF CONGRESS, PRESENTED TO MR. HASKINS AND MR. SELLS IN APPRECIATION OF THEIR SERVICES TO THE GOVERNMENT.

XV

The investigation at Washington, with its long, close study and infinite detail, was at last completed. For nearly two years Mr. Haskins and Mr. Sells had been in daily conference and collaboration, and the strong friendship and confidence that had grown between them made a partnership seem almost inevitable. During the closing weeks of their labors on behalf of the Commission, they talked much of their future plans, and on March 4, 1895, they opened an office at No. 2 Nassau Street, New York, under the firm name of Haskins & Sells.

Among the first engagements that came to the partners was an examination of the methods of accounting at Vassar College. This work came through Mr. S. D. Coykendall, one of the trustees of the college. Mr. Coykendall or his son has been a client of the firm since that time.

The engagements that followed covered services for the Government, States, municipalities, banks, trust companies, insurance companies, street and steam railways, and mercantile and industrial organizations. The familiarity of the two members of the firm with all the problems and intricacies of railroad management and accounting brought to them many calls for service.

The practice ended its first year with a gross in-come amounting to $15,000, and increased annually about fifty per cent over the previous year until the income approximated $400,000, the high-water mark which was reached at the time of Mr. Haskins' death. Practice from the very beginning was general, al-though there were some special investigations for public interests. The first was for the City of New York, under the administration of Mayor Strong, who was elected on a reform ticket. There was also municipal accounting for several smaller cities: New Rochelle, N. Y., Houston, Texas, Atlanta, Ga., Oklahoma City, Okla., Kingston, N. Y., and others.

XVI

Perhaps the most important and interesting work undertaken by the young firm was an audit and restatement of the special assessment accounts of the City of Chicago from the time of the great fire, 1871, to 1891, an extensive work of its kind which it was estimated would cost the city $65,000, and require about ten months labor with a large force of accountants. It proved to be so arduous and complicated that it occupied approximately two years and cost $174,000. The City of Chicago paid only the amount of the estimate—$65,000, leaving the balance of $109,000 to be absorbed by Haskins & Sells. About the same time, the partners had also an engagement for the installation of a new system of general accounts for Chicago, which proved to be a profitable piece of work.

Never was any city in such dire need of the kind of service which Haskins & Sells could render as was the City of Chicago. Compared with it, the condition of the accounting methods of the National Government were almost perfection. Chicago had grown with marvelous rapidity, swallowing up adjacent villages and hamlets, which she gorged without digestion. In the words of Mr. Haskins, "pre-existing organizations, however, have been left intact, and other corporations, with municipal powers, have been added; thus within the territory of Chicago is now found an aggravation of Cook County chaos such as no man has yet been able to describe.

"Nobody, for example, agrees with anybody else as to how many taxing bodies there are in Chicago. Professor Gray says nineteen—peculating, wasting, quarreling, fighting, and constantly appealing to the legislature and to the courts. Mr. Giles says three distinct governments, with a dozen different taxing powers, which, for the purpose of raising insufficient funds, unequally distribute burdens of taxation. The lawyers of the Civic Federation sum up twenty municipal or quasi-municipal corporations, some partially dependent on the city machinery; others entirely independent. The recent report to the Merchants' Club says 'There are at least twenty-one different taxing bodies in the city. It has been said that one may take his stand on any street corner in Chicago and find himself amenable to at least five different governments, and that each one takes him and filches him and gives him nothing in return.' "

This was only a single illustration of the chaos that reigned in Chicago when Mr. Haskins and his forty assistants, representing the firm of Haskins & Sells, took up the work. What they accomplished can be seen in the report of the comptroller of the City of Chicago, after the new system, based on their recommendations, had been in operation one year. The features of the new systems, as there set forth, are as follows:

"(1) Uniformity in accounting methods; (2) concentration of the accounting in the comptroller's office; (3) collection of all revenue by the city collector; (4) daily remittances; (5) monthly reports and balances between the comptroller and all departments; (6) monthly financial report of the comptroller; (7) organization of an audit bureau and of a methodical plan of auditing by officers and employes retained especially for that purpose and independent of all departments; (8) accruement of revenues on the general books of the city, where they will always be evident as obligations due the city until paid; (9) approval of all contracts and requisitions for supplies by the comptroller, to prevent departments from incurring liabilities in excess of appropriations; (10) the issuance of all fiscal stationery, forms, and receipts consecutively numbered by the comptroller and holding the departments responsible for their use or cancellation; (11) the use of graduated stubs or coupon receipts to check the collection of money; (12) the establishment of a complete chain of accounting, from the inception of revenue or expense, throughout the various branches of the city, to the comptroller's office, where all the accounting is finally centralized."

The report said further: "As the result of the better administrative control effected, we learn that the revenues of the city, from direct and indirect taxation, fees of departments, etc., have increased nearly a million dollars, while the permanent saving of administration expenses have been reduced over seventy thousand dollars a year."

XVII

In 1896, when the business of the new firm was about a year old, the Legislature of the State of New York, at the request of the accountants of the State and for their protection, passed an act "to regulate the profession of public accountants." This act provided for a class of public expert accountants to be known as "certified public accountants" and to have the exclusive right to use the three letters "C. P. A." after their names; and it authorized the Regents of the University to establish examinations and to issue certificates of recognition to those who proved themselves capable and expert and fulfilled other necessary requisites. This certificate was to be accorded only to those at least twenty-five years of age, of good moral character, who had had three years' satisfactory experience in the practice of accounting, one of which must have been in the office of an expert public accountant.

Absorbed in their new firm, with its exacting demands on their time and energy, the two partners had taken no direct part in securing the new legislation, though they were in closest sympathy with the aims to be accomplished. Shortly after the passage of the act, Mr. Sells had to make a business trip up the State and decided to stop off at Albany and have a talk

with Dr. Melvil Dewey about certain details of the
working of the new law.

In the interview that followed, mention was made
of the Board of Examiners, and Mr. Sells instantly
felt that there was one man who should be a member
of the Board and that man was Charles Waldo Haskins. He told Dr. Dewey of Mr. Haskins' standing
in the profession, his ideals, his accomplishments, his
splendid record of achievement, and his special fitness
for this post of honor and responsibility. Dr. Dewey
was impressed with the genuine enthusiasm of the
plea, but said that the matter would be decided at a
meeting of the Board of Regents on the morning of
the day following when the three examiners would be
appointed. He regretted that he would not be able
to help Mr. Haskins' cause as it was necessary that
the names of candidates should be accompanied by
strong endorsements presenting their claims and the
time was too short to secure them. Mr. Sells was not
in the least dismayed by this finality, but gave no sign
to Dr. Dewey, as he thanked him for his courteous
attention and took his leave.

Mr. Sells thought out instantly a rapid and effective means of meeting this eleventh-hour situation.
He called up one of his lieutenants in New York by
long distance telephone, told him just what was
needed, gave him a list of the men to see, told him
what to say to each, and urged him to have telegrams
sent to Albany giving their endorsement of Mr. Haskins as a member of the Board of Examiners. The
next morning when the Regents met, there lay before

them a stack of telegrams from the most influential men in New York, representing the largest interests and institutions of the city. So overwhelming was the endorsement that Mr. Haskins was unanimously elected by the Regents. The other two members of the Board of Examiners were Mr. Frank Broaker and Mr. Charles E. Sprague.

At the first meeting of the Examiners, Mr. Haskins was made president, a position he retained until his death. In the spring of 1897, he helped to organize the New York State Society of Certified Public Accountants and became its first president.

XVIII

Soon there came suggestions for the founding of a school of accountancy. It seemed to originate in many minds simultaneously, for a profession carried with it as a natural corollary, an institution of training for that profession. The Board of Examiners felt the need of it; the New York State Society discussed it freely; Mr. Haskins and Mr. Sells talked much of it and made many tentative plans for transforming it from a mere idea into a living actuality; and other devoted members of the profession were in close sympathy with the movement.

At the November, 1899, meeting of the New York State Society of Certified Public Accountants, Mr. Henry R. M. Cook introduced a motion requesting the President to confer with the Trustees of New York University for the purpose of arranging for the establishment of a class for a technical course of study in the science of accounts, finance, economics, business practice, commercial law, and so forth, and, moreover, the President was invited to co-operate with kindred societies in the State for the purpose of successfully carrying out the resolution. On December 11, 1899, Mr. Haskins, President of the State Society, wrote to Chancellor Henry M. MacCracken, requesting a conference with the object of effecting an agreement for the establishment of the desired technical course of study.

In the story of the later interview with Chancellor MacCracken, it must not be understood that this was the first effort made to secure the co-operation of an American university and, because the idea was a good one and represented a real need, that it had but to be brought before the attention of the proper authorities to be at once welcomed with open arms. The idea of the course in accounting had earnestly and eloquently been presented to other leading educational institutions, but they disdainfully drew closer around them the robes of their sacred scholasticism, that they might not be tainted by the desecrating touch of commercialism, and, like the Pharisee of old, passed by on the other side. It requires vision to realize a great truth in the dawn of its youth and to accept it; it requires vision to fight for such a truth and to battle on courageously till victory is achieved.

XIX

The story of one part of the struggle for an educational institution of accountancy cannot be told better than in Mr. Haskins' own words: "A history of the origin of this school would be the history of accountancy, especially in America, and of the movement in behalf of higher commercial education whose wave is now washing the shores of the United States. Most of you are familiar with the laws regulating the profession of accountancy, and with the efforts of the better class of accountants to secure a solid educational and social basis for the profession, as well as with the rise and growth of what is coming to be known as the profession of administration—represented by men of marked executive ability, whose bent of mind is toward the comprehensive and detailed control of affairs. From these sources has come the two-fold demand which has been recognized by the New York University in the establishment of the new school. The more immediate story, however, of its origin is too good to be lost.

"Chancellor MacCracken, in his last annual report, reminded the Council that the seventieth anniversary of the University would occur in October, 1900, and suggested the celebration of this septuagesimal in some way which might at the same time signalize the advent of the twentieth century of our era. Consciously or unconsciously, this suggestion was a pre-intimation of the establishment of the eighth teaching institution under the University. Shortly after the appearance of the Chancellor's report, a committee representing a large number of leading professional accountants of the State of New York laid before him an outline of a plan for a school or college of accountancy, emphasizing also the desirability of University control of such a school, with a view to placing the profession upon a proper educational and moral basis of efficiency and reliability.

"The matter was presented to the Council of the University, and was duly considered by a special committee, consisting of Dr. MacCracken, Messrs. William F. Havemeyer, William S. Opdyke, William M. Kingsley, and James G. Cannon. Consultation led to further suggestion; the movement for higher commercial education received due consideration; to accountancy was added commerce, and to these finance; the practical, every-day applications of the broad science of economics were canvassed as only men of large economic thought and experience are able to cope with the subject; and on July 28 the petitioners were officially notified of the decision legalizing the foundation of the new college, to be known as the New York University School of Commerce, Accounts, and Finance.

"Thus, in the morning watch of the dawning century, comes into existence an institution of professional learning fitly characteristic of the age and memorial of an epoch in the life of a great administrative educational corporation."

XX

With the simplicity and modesty that seems to be
the hallmark of the men who do the big work of the
world, Mr. Haskins makes no reference to himself
in this narrative; one might suppose him but the im-
partial historian of this important movement, while
to him, more than to any other one man, is due the
credit for carrying it through.

On Tuesday, October 2, 1900, the new school—the
first of its kind in the world—began its pioneer work
in the University building in Washington Square,
New York. A number of excellent speeches were delivered by Chancellor MacCracken, Colonel Sprague,
and other members of the faculty. The Dean of the
School, Mr. Haskins, after a few general remarks,
gave his first lecture as Professor of the History of
Accountancy. There were about fifty matriculants
in attendance at this opening session.

It may be of interest to note here that shortly after
Mr. Haskins had been elected Dean, the University
conferred on him the degree of Master of Arts. The
Chancellor told him that, because of his relation to
the school that had to do with business and not with
the recognized sciences, his acknowledgment of the
degree in English would be acceptable. Mr. Haskins,
however, preferred to conform to the traditions of the

University and gracefully acknowledged in Latin the honor conferred on him.

What may be termed the intellectual and ethical platform of the School may be given in Mr. Haskins' own words: "No attempt will be made in the school to foster the notion that commerce or accountancy is a royal road to wealth, or to leisure, or to unmerited social position; but in addition to the intellectual qualifications of talent for observation, power of perception, patience of investigation, presence of mind, judgment, reflection, order and method, aptitude for calculation, abstraction, memory, mental activity and steadiness, which it is hoped the student will possess in some fair degree, the moral virtues of honesty, candor, firmness, prudence, truth, justice, economy, temperance, liberality, politeness, good temper, self control, and perseverence will be inculcated as necessary to his own personal welfare and the stability of the business world."

Some of the early struggles are given by Mr. Leon Brummer, who had been a devoted ally in the movement to get the School organized, and was a teacher from the beginning: "The students were permitted to enter certain classes of the Law School, and other than the teachers of those Law School classes, there were but six teachers of accountancy, one teacher of economics, and one other instructor. I know that, judging from my own class, the accounting knowledge of the students was so ungraded; the knowledge of the teacher and his ability to teach was so uncertain; and the confidence of the scholars, who were continually asking for instruction in higher accountancy, was so wanting, that nothing but the persistent efforts and the personal encouragement and glorious example of Charles Waldo Haskins kept the School from following in the footpaths of those which had gone before.

"As I look upon this scene and upon the inexperience of the early teachers, the absolute absence of guiding precedents, the want of literature, the eagerness of all those students of more than average intelligence for instruction in accounting, it is not at all surprising that the older and unschooled accountants of today fear to undertake the duties of a teacher in this School, but leave this task mostly for the men who have been graduated from the School."

There was no endowment fund to render the way partially easy by doing away with the financial problem which, with its insistent worry and wearing down of mental energy, keeps men from giving their minds fully and freely to their work. The first professors and instructors, who were nearly all practicing certified public accountants, gave their time and abilities almost gratis and at a real personal sacrifice. It was with them largely a labor of love and a fine spirit of devotion and helpfulness to their profession. The sessions of the School, contrary to all accepted traditions, were held in the late afternoons and in the evenings. The majority of the students were self-supporting, being occupied for the greater part of the day in some line of activity for the purpose of making money to help them through their course.

Despite all the hardships, struggles, discouragements, and obstacles, the new venture conquered and flourished and within a few years this, the youngest School in the University, had the largest enrollment of students. It not only performed fine, loyal, direct service to the profession in the number of young men it trained to take their places with splendid equipment and high ideals in the ranks of certified public accountants, but the School itself became an exemplar and an inspiration to other schools, more or less similar, started in other parts of the country.

XXI

In 1900, Mr. Haskins spent some months in an extensive trip abroad. During this time he devoted considerable time to the study of European accountancy as connected with higher commercial education. He was deeply interested in the history of accounting, tracing it back almost to primitive man, through all of the great civilizations down to the present. Business, trade, commerce, even in their earliest phases, presuppose as an accompaniment some method of keeping tallies or accounts. From the notched stick, the knotted string, or the scratched piece of clay, up to the finest and most elaborate modern system of keeping accounts is a wondrous process of evolution, as true and logical as the evolution to which Darwin, Wallace, Spencer, and other scientists devoted so great a part of their lives.

To some, the history of accounting might seem a heavy, dry-as-dust subject, to be studied as a painful duty as part of a curriculm. Those who think thus have never had the pleasure of listening to Mr. Haskins' lectures, addresses, and informal talks. Accounts, in some form or other, connote the interdependence and co-operation of man. Away back in the earliest years, when the earth was young and man had to exchange his labor or his possessions for

71

some concrete thing of another, and later when he began to give credit or to require it, some method of keeping track of the transactions became necessary, and at that moment came the dawn of accountancy. Mr. Haskins loved his subject and pored over countless volumes for interesting bits in the history of its evolution as found incidentally in the story of other peoples and other times. When he came across anything that was new, striking, or illuminating, he jotted it down in his notes with as genuine a pleasure as that of an enthusiastic philatelist adding a newly-acquired rare stamp to his collection.

His first lecture, at the opening of the School of Commerce, Accounts, and Finance on October 2, 1890, the beginning of his course in the history of accounting, was merely introductory. He said, among other things, as showing his realization of the far-reaching importance of the study of history:

"Accounting, as a progressive science, must be the same yesterday, today, and tomorrow, except that as a development it is older and wiser as time goes on. But how shall we go about this search into the labyrinth of former times? Where shall we find these severed fibres that may be twisted into the warp and woof which in turn may be woven into the fabric— the history of accountancy? Accounting, we know, is involved in the history of nations—in the more general history of civilization, in that of commerce, of banking, of education, of mathematics, of language, and a hundred others, so that in the study of these general and special histories we may hope to find, here and there, notices more or less extended of private and governmental accounts and methods of accounting. Biography is another source of history; folk-lore, poetry, drama, tales, and the like are a species of literature in which many a gem of our past lies hidden."

One may gather, from little hints dropped here and there in his lectures and his addresses before societies and other organizations that, despite his realization of the appalling amount of detail and research necessary to write an elaborate history of accounting, Mr. Haskins cherished the hope that sometime, somewhere, he would accomplish this work. In speaking to his classes of having begun to collect information on the history of accountancy he said: "In this, however, as in all our study, we must be co-workers, and if at any time any reader of any book shall find any line of fact that may be woven into our history, I trust I may have the benefit of his acquisition."

XXII

All big men of action and of achievement are dreamers; they have a vision of larger things that they wish to accomplish; their faces are set steadily forward and the future appears rosy with thoughts of golden deeds. But the busy days of Mr. Haskins, filled with his professional duties, his collegiate responsibilities, and the other constant demands on his time and energy, left him no leisure period free for the realization of his dream.

With men of achievement, one never asks why they did not accomplish more; one only wonders how they found time to do so much. So it was with Charles Waldo Haskins. As a writer he was clear, scholarly, entertaining, and convincing, and whatever he wrote on any topic showed a wide acquaintance with the classics and a familiarity with the best of European as well as British and American writers. His lectures on accounting suggest a vast amount of research, yet all so perfectly assimilated, so blended by his own individuality and his own interpretation, that they have no obtrusion of the pedantry one so often associates with scholarship.

He traveled extensively in all parts of the United States and Europe, but on every return from a trip he was more enthusiastic about the City of New York which he loved with a devotion that is more common

in the heart of an adopted son of the metropolis than
in a native-born. He took a deep interest in local
politics and was an active worker for good government. He had no longing for public offices, and on
occasions when he was urged to accept some post of
honor and trust under the city government, declared
that he would not accept even the highest position in
the gift of its citizens—that of Mayor of New York
—as it would remove him from the field of his life
work, accountancy. No matter what was the pres-
sure of the cares and responsibilities of his profession,
which had for him the sacredness of a mission, a call
to make an address or to write an article on accountancy had for him the insistence and finality that a
command to visit the king has on citizens of the mon-
archies of Europe.

Mr. Haskins was of stalwart physique, vital, puls-
ing with health and good spirits, kindly, cordial and
hearty in manner, magnetic in personality, making
friends readily and holding them strongly, as was attested by the popularity he won in the twenty or more
clubs, societies, and associations of which he was a
member.

In his thirty-third year he was married to Miss
Henrietta Havemeyer, a daughter of Albert Havemeyer, a leading citizen and merchant of New York
and of the family so well-known in the financial and
social history of the city. Mrs. Haskins' uncle, the
Honorable Willian F. Havemeyer, was New York's
most popular mayor and was twice the incumbent of
that office.

It seems a bit paradoxical that a man whose special genius of mind and thought ran to figures and finance should have had so fine and natural an artistic taste and ability. In his first trip to Europe in his youth he studied art under the best teachers in Paris, and several of his early productions, still preserved, show unusual artistic talent. He had in his home a collection of paintings which gave him great pleasure. Though not large in number, they were carefully selected by him and reveal the fineness of his critical acumen and the depth of his appreciation of the beautiful in art.

In all his manifold interests and activities, Mr. Haskins continued to be a vital factor in the firm of Haskins & Sells, which was rapidly making its way, strengthening its personnel, opening new offices, widening its field of business and influence, and establishing and sustaining the sound basic principles that have governed its organization in all the later years of its fuller success.

XXIII

On Friday evening, January 2, 1903, Mr. Haskins gave a dinner in one of the private dining rooms of the Manhattan Club, New York, to members of the committee on uniform municipal accounting of the National Municipal League. He was seemingly in the best of health, cordial and hearty in his welcome to his guests, bright and charming in his conversation, and, in the business discussion that followed, modestly guided and controlled a decision when he seemed only incidentally to suggest. The next day he was taken seriously ill with pneumonia and on the 9th of January the end came. The news of the death of Mr. Haskins was a sudden, startling shock to those nearest to him in his social and business relations and who but a few days before had seen him in the best of health; to all who knew him his death was a personal grief and a real loss. He was buried on January 11, the anniversary of his fifty-first birthday, having died in the prime of his life and powers.

From all parts of the country came letters and telegrams of condolence and sympathy to his widow and his two daughters, Ruth and Noeline, and to his business partners in Haskins & Sells who lost, in his passing, an associate, a loyal friend, and constant inspiration and guide. The multifold activities of his life were shown in the many angles from which the press discussed his career, and by the many societies and organizations that sent representatives to the funeral services, reverently to pay the last honors of respect and love to his memory.

No book written by Mr. Haskins was published during his lifetime, but shortly after his death two volumes of his work appeared. The first was a handbook of family finance, entitled "How to Keep Household Accounts" and dedicated to the author's daughter, Ruth. It gave in a simple, conversational way, with the charm of an entertaining style, the principles of accounting in relation to domestic economy, finance, administration, and the other sciences of social life. Its six chapters covered domestic economy, household accounts, the home account book, the balance sheet, budget, vouchers and inventory, and the bank account.

The second book, published in the year following, collected a number of his speeches and addresses under the title "Business Education and Accountancy." It was edited by Dr. Frederic A. Cleveland of the Wharton School of Finance and Commerce of the University of Pennsylvania, who also wrote the introduction and the sympathetic and appreciative biographical sketch. This book is a real contribution to the literature of accountancy and contains a treatment of the following subjects: business training, the scope of banking education, the possibilities of the profession of accountancy as a moral and educational force, the growing need for higher accountancy, the place of the science of accounts in collegiate commercial education, history of accountancy (an introduction), accountancy in Babylonia and Assyria, and the municipal accounts of Chicago.

XXIV

When Mr. Haskins passed away, he was still young —young in years, for he was only fifty-one years of age, and young in vitality, energy, ideals, optimism, courage, and the zest of life which keeps some men from ever growing old. No man who does real work for the world ever sees the full fruitage of his efforts. There is always a larger harvest than is visible to him at any time during his life-time; he does not realize the seeding of purpose, initiative, influence, and inspiration that mean constant new harvests after he is no longer present to see and to know, and when he is but a golden sacred memory to those who have known him best and loved him best.

Thus it was with Charles Waldo Haskins. The impetus he gave to the profession of accountancy can never be fully realized. By work and act he ever unselfishly sought its progress and development. The New York University School of Commerce, Accounts, and Finance has grown and flourished beyond any dream of his. The firm of Haskins & Sells, founded on the broad principles of fine ethics which expressed the ideals and vision of both Mr. Haskins and his friend and partner, Mr. Sells, has moved steadily forward to larger things and wider lines of usefulness in accord with what they both dreamed together and wrought into achievement.

The conception that Mr. Haskins had of his profession cannot be better given than in his own words:

"The ideal conception by the profession itself of its true mission, a conception from within and not dependent upon extraneous exigencies, places accountancy far outside the pale of ordinary callings, and sets it upon a platform of its own as a learned profession, self-impelled to culture, to moral enlargement, and to scientific attainment, and lays a basis of confidence for every business enterprise that in professional accountancy there is a self-centered soul of economic truth."

XXV

On Saturday evening, December 17, 1910, nearly eight years after the death of Mr. Haskins, a memorable meeting was held in the University building in Washington Square, New York. The occasion for the notable gathering was the unveiling of a bronze memorial tablet in honor of the life and services of Mr. Haskins, the first Dean of the School of Commerce, Accounts, and Finance. The tablet, the work of Rudulph Evans, a young sculptor who had recently won a medal of honor at the Paris Salon, was the affectionate and appreciative gift of the Class of 1910 and other alumni of the School, and of the friends of Dean Haskins.

In all the addresses, made by well-known accountants and men prominent in the world of business, was to be noted a deep and sincere recognition of the character and personality of Mr. Haskins, as well as an appreciation and realization of his work as an educator and his loyal and devoted service to the profession he loved, and labored so zealously to advance.

Professor Leon Brummer, Secretary of the New York State Society of Certified Public Accountants in 1900, told of the efforts incident to the founding of the School and of the part that Mr. Haskins had taken in this work and in its administration during

the trying first years. Dr. John H. MacCracken,
Acting Chancellor of New York University, discussed
the share of the University in education preparatory
to accountancy and other business professions. Mr.
Frank A. Vanderlip, then President of the National
City Bank, in a vivid and telling way summed up the
ideals of Mr. Haskins in relation to accountancy and
to the education that was essential to all who desired
to enter the profession. The Honorable Myron T.
Herrick, ex-Governor of Ohio, delivered a most interesting and thoughtful address on the work of Mr.
Haskins and on the need of university training for
business men.

On behalf of the members of the Class of 1910,
Mr. H. M. James presented the tablet, with sincere
appreciation of the generous co-operation of all those
who had made the gift possible. Dean Johnson received it for the School, and the tablet was unveiled
by Miss Dorothy Sells, the daughter of Elijah W.
Sells, Mr. Haskins' partner and closest friend.

No one who was privileged to be present on that
evening will ever forget it. The audience was in many
ways a distinguished one, not only because many of
the leading men in the profession of accountancy were
present, but because as one's eyes wandered over the
large audience, giving close attention, one noted with
pleasure the number of men present who counted as
vital and controlling powers in the worlds of finance
and business. There was a remarkable atmosphere
of simplicity, sincerity, and dignity about the meeting; a spirit of fine, grateful genuine appreciation, as

though all present felt the privilege of honoring Dean Haskins. But at the same time there was a note of impressive seriousness, because their gathering together in this manner emphasized the sadness of the fact that Mr. Haskins was no longer with them.

Because of the importance of the addresses made on this occasion, the illuminating side-lights they cast on the character and services of Charles Waldo Haskins, and their vital part in the history of accountancy, it has been deemed wise to give them here in full.

Part II

ADDRESSES DELIVERED ON THE OCCASION OF THE PRESENTATION TO THE NEW YORK UNIVERSITY SCHOOL OF COMMERCE, ACCOUNTS, AND FINANCE, OF THE CHARLES WALDO HASKINS MEMORIAL TABLET.

SPEAKERS

MYRON T. HERRICK, *Ex-Governor of Ohio.*
JOHN H. MacCRACKEN, Ph.D.
FRANK A. VANDERLIP, A.M., LL.D.
LEON BRUMMER, C. P. A.
H. M. JAMES, B. C. S.
JOSEPH FRENCH JOHNSON, D.C.S., LL.D.

UNIVERSITY TRAINING FOR BUSINESS MEN

By Myron T. Herrick

Ex-Governor of Ohio

The whole world follows, with unabated interest, any tale of human life that portrays the career of a young man. The story of his achievement is, and ever has been, among the leading subjects of the historian and among the favorite themes of the novelist. In his tens of thousands of lives are written, in poetry and prose, the history and romance of society. Therefore, to him who points out the way of success to the young man, and who labors constantly and unselfishly to supply the essentials of success in any field of human endeavor, laurels are unstintingly given by a grateful people, as a public recognition of his right to a high place among those to whom the world is indebted. Such a man was Charles Waldo Haskins.

His experience taught him the importance to a young man, about to enter a business career, of having a broad foundation of thorough, systematic training. He gave freely of his time and experience to this end. In line with his convictions, he assisted, to the utmost of his ability, in the establishment and upbuilding of this splendid New York University School

of Commerce, Accounts, and Finance. He was the
first Dean of the School; and the success that School
already has attained is striking proof of the sound-
ness of his ideas and of the permanent character of
the plans that he did so much to work out. It is,
therefore, eminently appropriate that the memory of
Mr. Haskins should be perpetuated, and that this
bronze tablet—a memorial of his life and services—
should be presented to the University on this occasion
of the tenth anniversary of the School.

The New York University School of Commerce,
Accounts, and Finance, early in its career, has com-
pletely justified its existence. It has an important
mission to perform. Its achievements are prophetic
of its permanent and constantly-growing utility. As
constituted today, the industry of the country must
have at its head men of trained efficiency. The day
of the Jack-of-all-trades is gone, never to return. The
man who knows, not the man who guesses, is the only
one who now need apply. The School of Commerce,
Accounts, and Finance is playing an important part
in supplying such men.

Industrial and commercial education is not one-
sided. The employer and the young man anxious
to fit himself for a successful business career are equal-
ly and vitally concerned. The employer's success de-
pends upon having efficient men about him. The
president of a railroad, bank, or of an industrial or
commercial enterprise, who is conscious of new conditions, will not surround himself with untrained men,
whose capacity is limited to routine clerical duties.

Competition demands that the employer have efficient, well-trained labor in the shop and in the office. He must have about him men whose training has made them capable of successfully assuming larger and larger responsibilities. For the success of the young man anticipating a business career, it is essential that he be so trained that he can see and grasp the opportunities that will come to him. If he is untrained and inaccurate and lacking in efficiency, he will be of indifferent value to his employer, and in the crucible of today's competition, must sooner or later find himself on the "scrap heap."

In the past twenty-five years, the manner and method of doing business has materially changed. The requirements of efficient service are now imperative in up-to-date, successful, militant business. A quarter of a century ago, special training was not thought necessary, or even desirable, for those about to enter business; education, commonly, was considered a waste of time. Success came easily to those who possessed imagination, determination, and industry. Practical experience then took the place of special training. Industrial relations were simple, and the scope, even of the great industrial enterprises, was very limited as compared with that of the great corporation of to-day. Then industry demanded of a young man simply those qualities that may be developed by experience; today, industry demands that the young man possess an accurate scientific knowledge of principles, in order that he may make the most of later experience. Then the average manufacturer operated a small plant, and sold to a local market. The details of such a business were simple; experience and bluff could supply all the preparation necessary to success. Today, business has become so highly developed that these qualifications alone, will not suffice. The manufacturer now operates in a continent-wide or world-wide market. His business is directly or indirectly affected by industrial conditions outside of his immediate neighborhood, and it is sensitive to many social and political influences.

It is only within the last decade—practically within the life of this School—that the banker of America has come to appreciate the necessity of understanding the philosophy of his business. Banking is each day becoming more complicated—less of a trade and more of a science. The successful banker of tomorrow must know more than how to shave notes—the bare details of his business. He must be conversant with the history of banking; familiar with the general laws that govern financial phenomena. He should recognize his obligations and relations to the people outside the counter, and have some comprehension of things other than those incident to mere money-getting. He should be capable of anticiapting the tendency of industrial and financial movements of wide extent, that he may today begin preparations for the emergency of a year hence.

More and more the banker is being depended upon to maintain the financial equilibrium of the community. This requires a degree of intelligence rarely gained from mere experience. The American and State

Bankers' Associations and the American Institute of Banking have done much, in recent years, to inform themselves and the people of the necessity of currency reform, and to divert the "David Harum" banker from the realm of "horse trades" into broader fields of finance; but from the nature of these associations, the educational value of their work is limited. They can do little more than suggest, and stimulate the consideration of banking and financial problems along proper lines. They can never adequately supply the present-day demand for sound training in the theory and practice of banking. This can be secured only by following the systematic courses now offered by such institutions as this.

Not only does the young man going into business today have more difficult problems to decide, and more complex relations to understand, but his opportunity for gaining knowledge by experience is much less favorable than it was. Twenty-five years ago, the division of labor was not so minute as it is now. The activities of the young man in business were not then so narrowly confined. He had greater scope; his duties were much more varied, and he had an opportunity to understand the relation of his special duties to the whole enterprise. Experience was then much more valuable as a training school. In the highly-developed industries of today, experience is apt to be confined to the doing of routine work, which, unless the employe has a well-trained mind, makes him an unreasoning cog in a large machine, and prevents him from appreciating even the significance of the work that he is doing, or its relation to the enterprise.

Business men now recognize the importance of thorough industrial and commercial education, and they seek young men especially trained for the part they are to take. Formerly, little attention was paid to the qualifications of the "new boy" other than to know that he was of good character and industrious. Now he must have a foundation of education on which may be built a proprietor. The "new boy" of the right sort does not stand long on the lower rung of the ladder.

Industrial and commercial education has an importance to society even greater than it has to the business man and those about to become business men. The most serious problems that confront the State and the Nation today are those intimately connected with industry. The regulation of public service corporations, so that every interest concerned, the stockholders, and the people, shall be properly conserved; the granting of franchises by municipalities; the taxation of industrial and public service corporations and the conservation of our natural resources, are all problems that for proper solution demand special knowledge and special training, and are too closely connected with the welfare of the people to be made the playthings of demagogues and self-seeking politicians.

The statute books of the State and the Nation are cluttered with unwise and vicious laws relating to all of these questions. Some of these laws originated in good intention; some in the desire of self-aggrandizement; mostly, however, they are the result of legislation by those who did not know—they simply guessed. These questions will be properly settled only when public opinion is guided by those fitted by training and experience to understand them. Your phenomenal success here is largely due to the fact that the public believes you give your young men that sort of training.

Of equal importance to the demand for efficient service in public affairs is the need for conscientiously-trained men in newspaper work. The young man to be so trained should not be self-selected. The great newspaper-reading public's voracious appetitie for news should not be fed on adulterated food, and the newspaper men who furnish it should be amenable to the pure-food laws, and as severely punished as the man who insults a healthy stomach with sanded sugar. The newspapers of the country are the greatest of all powers for good or evil. Most newspapers take their responsibilities seriously, and endeavor to promote the general welfare; others cater to temporary popular prejudice and clamor, and make no attempt either to direct or reflect public opinion, unless it pays to do so. Such newspapers do not hesitate to misrepresent those in public or private life, or to distort and color news, if, by so doing, they can serve their own mercenary purpose.

This University, in its school for training men for newspaper work, has entered a fruitful field, for in no other division of industry is there greater need for men possessed of a high sense of their responsibility, and conscientiously and thoroughly trained in the theory and practice of their work. As society becomes more and more complex in its makeup, the newspaper constantly requires a higher order of intelligence. It is impossible for an untrained mind adequately to grasp the meaning of events and correctly to appreciate the news value and social importance of the day's happenings. To sift all the news of the day and to give to the public only that which is of real importance, requires great ability and integrity. For such work, experience is not a sufficient teacher. The young man about to take up journalism as a life work needs such training in the ethics, theory, and practice of the profession as can be secured only by doing special collegiate work. * * * * * * *

In this country the prodigality of nature has developed a wasteful disposition among the people, and heretofore nature has borne the burden of the waste. Success has come to us so easily that we have become carelessly confident. We have now exhausted much of the surplus of the natural wealth of the country, and from now on our industrial and commercial enterprises must be conducted along different lines if we are not to fall behind in the race for commercial supremacy. In the future, a large part of the profits of industry must come from efficient, thorough organization, from the use of the most economical methods of production, and from the application of highly-trained minds to industrial and commercial problems; therefore, there will be an ever-increasing demand for young men who have received a systematic industrial education.

The importance to the community of schools like this cannot be over-estimated. It is to such institutions that the country must look for the trained men—men on whom will rest the responsibility of developing to the utmost the industrial and commercial possibilities of the country.

To the men who still hold the reins in America has been accorded the privilege of living in a momentous and stirring age. They have been builders and not destroyers; men of conception and achievement who have advanced civilization and lifted the entire fabric of society to a higher plane. They have, at times, counteracted revolutionary forces that threatened the life of the Republic. They are men mostly educated in the hard school of experience, but whose patriotism, while it may at times have been diluted, has not been blighted by the materialistic trend of the times. These men are destined, ere long, to leave behind a fair inheritance as the fruits of their labors; a marvelous trust to be administered by the men and boys who are now students in the schools and colleges throughout the land, and who happily are now awakening to the consciousness of the great responsibilities which shall soon become theirs.

While the men now in power have averted appalling crises, bridged chasms, scaled fortresses, and challenged the admiration of the world by marvelous achievements, the responsibilities awaiting these young men who are to step into their shoes are even greater. But to the young, courageous American, with his ability, genius, and delightful optimism, the path is not dark

and stormy; he has a chart of experience before him
more than two centuries old—if he will consult it—
on which he may clearly trace the successes and fail-
ures of kingdoms, empires, and republics, and profit
thereby. Meantime, it is in such as you that the hope
of the future lies.

ADDRESS AT THE UNVEILING OF THE HASKINS MEMORIAL TABLET

By John H. MacCracken, Ph.D.

Archbishop Chicele, who founded All Souls College at Oxford, made it a condition of his gift that the Fellows of the College should forever care for his tomb at Canterbury Cathedral. He died before the discovery of America and no tomb is more likely to receive perennial care, in the future as in the past, than the tomb of the wise ecclesiastic who rested his faith in the permanency of a school. Mr. Haskins left the School, of which he was one of the principal founders, no building and no endowment, nor is the School bound by any deed of gift to cherish his memory. His bequest to the School of Commerce, Accounts, and Finance was an idea, and because this idea has proved potent and fruitful beyond the most sanguine expectations, the students and friends of the School turn naturally to perpetuate his memory. The University authorities gladly accept the custody of this memorial, and wish me to express to those who have been instrumental in establishing it, their hearty appreciation of the thoughtfulness and generosity which have inscribed here the name of the first Dean, for coming generations of students to read and revere.

We trust that the bronze tablet unveiled this evening
will outlive the building in which it finds a temporary
home, and have a honored place in the statelier halls
which the generations will bring.

It has been said that the first rule for success is to
select the right grandfather. If you students and
alumni of the School of Commerce have shown wisdom
in selecting this School as your fostering mother, you
may congratulate yourselves also that this fostering
mother was the child of a man so clear in vision and
so strong in faith as Mr. Haskins. It was never my
good fortune, like the other speakers of the evening,
to know Mr. Haskins personally. At the time the
School was founded, I was in the West, enjoying the
wide perspective of the Missouri prairies. I recall,
however, that when I joined my father in the Catskills
in the summer of 1900, he outlined to me the plan
of the School and we discussed together the name
"Commerce, Accounts, and Finance." For ten years,
therefore, the name of Mr. Haskins has stood in my
mind for an idea rather than for a personality; and as
it is the idea as well as the man that we celebrate tonight, I leave to others the pleasant task of speaking
of Mr. Haskins as a friend, and will say a brief word
only regarding the idea for which his name stands.

I was struck by the fact in that early conversation
with the Chancellor, that Mr. Haskins and his associates who proposed the organization of the new School
were men more interested in substance than form.
They did not begin with a name and then decide what
the School was to do, but began with a concrete task

and permitted the organization to assume a form adapted to the task. As I understand it, those who proposed the organization of the School wanted first of all the help of an educational institution in creating and maintaining a new profession—the profession of certified public accountant, and secondly, they wanted instruction which should widen the outlook of young business men, enrich their lives, and fit them for the wider opportunities which modern industrial organization affords. I recall that the Chancellor said more than once that this School differed from all other university schools of business in that it had *"as its backbone,"* as he expressed it, the task of preparing men for a definite profession, the profession of the accountant. Mr. Haskins saw ten years ago what the rest of the world has come to see more clearly since—that the intricacies of modern corporate organizations and the multiplying of governmental activities were destined to create a new profession or give a new significance to one already existing in a minor way. Mr. Haskins probably did not foresee, nor could any one have foreseen at the time, the sudden growth of the demand on the part of the public for publicity of corporate affairs. He would have been an extraordinary prophet who could have predicted that this appetite, whetted by the gas and insurance investigations, would have become so insatiate in so short a time.

Just as the great corporations have created a new field for lawyers, giving them an opportunity to apply their trained brains to knotty business questions and to show business men how the thing can be done which they want done, so the creation of great corporations has created a new field for the man with expert financial knowledge, in interpreting to owners and stockholders and the public at large what it is that the corporation has done in carrying out the wishes of the business man in the way suggested by the lawyer, and what the result is in dollars and cents. Accounting, as Mr. Haskins expressed it, is the conning tower of modern business.

I am not gifted with prophetic insight and cannot foresee the future development of this profession. From my own experience, however, with the work of certified public accountants in the corporations with which I am connected, I see clearly one thing—that the future of the profession will depend on the intellectual power and breadth of the men who compose it. It is a comparatively simple thing to train men to prepare a report of the financial affairs of this, that, or the other corporation, according to a formal routine laid down in the accountant's office. It is a much more difficult thing to secure accountants who have had such preliminary training that they show the same analytical power possessed by a great corporation lawyer, and are able to adapt their methods to the specific problems and necessities of the particular corporation. No man of limited training can do this. It requires imagination to know what term to substitute for capital in a school like this which has no capital. It requires sagacity born of a wide experience and considerable reflection to pick out the important factors of a business and distinguish the essential points of view from the unessential points for the managers and for the stockholders. Accountancy as a profession has seemed too ready to give up the task of attempting to analyze corporation reports and certify to their accuracy, preferring the easier task of preparing a report of its own in accordance with fixed formulae, thus reducing the risk of error in the report and minimizing the amount of intense analytical mental activity which the examiner must exercise. To let some one else do the thinking may make a profession safe; it will never make it great. I see far enough ahead, therefore, to realize that Mr. Haskins has left us a larger task than we have yet been able to perform. In Mr. Haskins' own words, "so far we have just begun to approach the foot of the professional ladder. But as we look up and ask for further educational guidance, we realize that we have come to a lonesome place where few meet us, and these but newcomers and inquirers like ourselves."

For one thing, I should like to see the School of Commerce provided with endowments, so that it could do what the new government commercial school of Japan does—limit the number of its students in accountancy to 200, selecting these as the best qualified from among a thousand applicants. I should like to see the course of study made so intensive and extensive, that the possession of a degree from the School would be *prima facie* evidence that the man could do any of the tasks of an able certified public accountant in a superior way. At the same time, I would not cut off the wider influence of the School, but would endeavor

to carry out Mr. Haskins' second idea of widening the
outlook and improving the efficiency of young business men.   Mr. Crane of Chicago has recently published a book to prove that America is all wrong, and
that money spent on higher education is all wasted.
He has given it the title, "The Utility of All Kinds
of Higher Schooling," but the fitter title would be,
"The Futility of All Higher Schooling."   He is quite
convinced that in the Crane Shops he has a better university than Mr. Rockefeller's millions can ever build.
But even Mr. Crane seems to believe in books and the
efficacy of the pen.   One of the tasks of this School
—a task for which Mr. Haskins himself pointed the
way in his book on "Business Education and Acccount-
ing"—is, and will continue to be, to describe business
processes in scientific terms, and to observe, classify,
and name the phenomena of modern business so that
the human mind may grasp them, discover their significance, and generalize regarding them.   It is aston-
ishing to find how little scientific knowledge we possess
of the great business world which is all about us.
That there exists here a fruitful field for university
research was recognized even in the early days of this
University, when provision was made in the original
plan for a professorship of commerce.   The task be-
longs pre-eminently to this School, because no place
in the world offers so great opportunities for such
study as this richest city in the world, itself an epitome
of the world's business.

As I have said, Mr. Haskins left no building and
no endowment to the School he was instrumental in

founding. He left, however, a fruitful idea, and unless the history of the world in all this generation is to differ from the history of the world in all other generations, this idea must eventually clothe itself with a home and with material substance. The record of the endowments of the University of Cambridge, England, shows that back in medieval days it was not uncommon for money to be left to the colleges and along with the money a chest to keep the money in. The chests outlasted the money, but none of them, unfortunately, developed the quality of the widow's barrel, and the money taken from the chest did not return. We trust that we shall not have to wait long for the adequate housing of the work of the School of Commerce, but better that we should have a fruitful, multiplying idea, which, at the end of ten years cries for more room, than that we should find ourselves at this time the possessors of an empty shell, its golden store all spent. It is, therefore, with sincere appreciation that the University joins in paying tribute to Mr. Haskins and his large part in the establishment of this School of Commerce, Accounts, and Finance; and as we recall the first Dean, we think of his ideal of perfect accountancy: "forethought, friendliness, artful getting at things, fire of reason, mathematical accuracy, adherence to truth."

EDUCATIONAL IDEALS OF CHARLES WALDO HASKINS

By Frank A. Vanderlip, A.M., LL.D.

Former President of the National City Bank of New York City

Two features of Charles Waldo Haskins' character stand out most clearly before me as I look back on the man and his work. First, he was filled with unselfish professional zeal; second, his eyes were turned to the future, not the past.

The last twenty years have seen the rise to deserved prominence of a new profession—that of the public accountant. I am sure that I represent the feeling of the great majority of business men when I say that the business world has watched the development of accountancy with keen interest and hope. We hoped that it would be instrumental in bringing to the front safer, more conservative, more certain business methods. We hoped that it would supply to each business executive more scientific and more accurate information on which to base the conduct of his own affairs. We hoped, most of all, that it would help to place the stamp of unquestioned honesty on enterprises that deserve that stamp; so that integrity might become more and more the most essential factor in winning business success.

Twenty years ago the realization of these hopes

through the agency of public accountants seemed a
far-distant thing. Public accountancy as a distinct
profession was well-established in England, but, outside a limited circle, had gained very little recognition
in this country. Many who called themselves public
accountants were lacking in the most elementary
requisites for their work; they had neither special
training nor special ability, and there were even instances where they were lacking in strict integrity.
Understand that I am far from imputing these de-
fects to the majority of public accountants of twenty
years ago; I mean only that as a body they had not yet
set up and made widely known to business men definite standards of knowledge and of honesty. Both
the science and the ethics of accountancy, as I understand it, were as yet unformulated.

As the first step in raising public accountancy to a
higher plane, it was necessary that a professional spirit
should be fostered; that a body of professional knowledge should be built; that professional standards of
conduct should be established. To help in accomplish-
ing these things was undoubtedly one of the controlling purposes of Mr. Haskins' life. He wished to
realize this purpose, not merely for his own sake, but
because it would make greater and more admirable
the profession of public accountancy. Of the many
steps that he took, guided by this purpose, I need
mention only his earnest advocacy of legal control of
the degree of Certified Public Accountant, and his
labors in organizing the School of Commerce, Accounts, and Finance.

Today the hopes which business men entertained twenty years ago, as to the possible services of the profession of public accountancy, have been largely realized. I do not mean that all the ideals of knowledge, efficiency, integrity, have been finally attained. I do mean that great progress toward these ideals has been made and that the ideals themselves are constantly rising. I can speak only as an outsider of what has been accomplished so far by the important profession of public accountancy and of what is yet to be accomplished. But judging from what I have observed, I feel certain that the profession is moving along the right lines; is establishing itself more and more firmly as an indispensable adjunct to American business; is building up through its associations and literature, and professional schools, a large and valuable body of knowledge; and, above all, is guided by the spirit of unity and honesty and efficiency which is the life of every profession.

Charles Waldo Haskins no doubt would be far from desiring sole credit—or even more credit than many other men—for these achievements. It is enough to say that he was among the first to adopt the professional ideals of public accountancy, and that he was always actuated by a true professional spirit.

The second characteristic of Mr. Haskins that I have mentioned—that his eyes were turned toward the future, not the past—perhaps explains why he devoted himself with so much zeal to the up-building of the profession of accountancy; it certainly explains why the last years of his life were taken up to a great extent with his duties as Dean of the School of Commerce, Accounts, and Finance.

Probably his first thought at the time when he and other accountants were just beginning to consider the possibility of organizing a professional school, on a university basis, for the training of public accountants, was that the profession of public accountancy would thereby be benefited.

But Charles Waldo Haskins was too big a man to confine his interests to a single object. He soon came to see that such a school would train men for executive work in banks, in mercantile and manufacturing establishments, as well as in public accounting offices. He saw, too, that no man can become a really capable public accountant merely by a specialized study of figures. The efficient public accountant must look in and through the figures, and see the facts, the methods, and the men which the figures represent. He must know something of organization, of transportation, of finance, if he is to be an intelligent accountant. And on the other hand, it is no less true that the average business man needs nothing more than a sound knowledge of accounting methods and principles.

Seeing these truths, Charles Waldo Haskins did not attempt to organize a school that should simply train technical accountants and do nothing else. He was too sensible, too far-sighted, to make such an error. He intended rather to organize a school in which should be brought together the information and the training that is most essential to all of us who are engaged in business affairs. This school, therefore, he called not "School of Accounting"; nor, if he had been primarily a financier, would he have called it "School of Finance"; like the broad-gauged man that he was, he approved the title "School of Commerce, Accounts, and Finance."

So far as I know, Mr. Haskins and his co-workers did not issue any statement or platform showing exactly what objects they had in mind in organizing the School. Judging from what I know of Mr. Haskins and of the School itself, I suspect that their platform, if they had prepared one, would have set forth their ambitions:

1. To provide for young men aspiring to become public accountants, a broad, well-rounded, professional training.

2. To provide for all other men engaged in business, a means for acquiring quickly, information as to sound business methods and principles.

3. To investigate business problems, and build up through investigation, a complete, systematic body of business knowledge—which might become, in the course of years, a true science of business.

4. To raise the standards of American business efficiency.

5. To inculcate sound and just views as to business morality.

Perhaps all these objects may not have been fully worked out in Dean Haskins' mind, but they must have been at least partially in his view. Otherwise, it is not conceivable that he could have guided the institution, during its earlier years, along such lines as to lead naturally to its later development.

The story of that development is familiar to all of us here. It is not merely a story of increasing numbers; it is a record of widening influence. We have seen other universities follow in the path which New York University blazed. We have seen indifference on the part of business men, as to university training for business, giving way to keen interest. We have seen some of the best thought of the country turn toward the scientific study of everyday business problems. In this great movement toward collecting and organizing business knowledge, the School of Commerce, Accounts, and Finance has borne a leading and always honorable part.

Looking back, it is hard to realize that only a little over ten years ago Dean Haskins presided over the first session of this School. There were forty students, I understand, at the beginning, against eleven hundred now. What is more important, there was indifference, derision, even determined opposition, at the beginning, as opposed to universal approval and support now. Dean Haskins worked in what we might call now the dark ages of higher commercial education. Though it was only ten years ago, yet the conditions and the problems that he faced, let us not forget, were in striking contrast to those of today.

We must all agree that Charles Waldo Haskins was largely instrumental in bringing about the rapid change. He started to do the work—started it courageously, confidently—because his eyes were fixed on the future. He fought against derision, inertia, misunderstanding, and partly conquered them. If he had lived, it would surely have gladdened his heart to see how effectively he had fought and how soundly he had built.

Our civic and social honors are rightly given first of all to the man who dares when others hold back—to the pioneer who advances from the point where others stand still. Charles Waldo Haskins was a pioneer; a man of foresight, of generous purposes, of unfailing courage. It is well that we have been brought together in this meeting to honor his memory.

THE INCEPTION AND FOUNDATION OF THE SCHOOL OF COMMERCE, ACCOUNTS, AND FINANCE

By Leon Brummer, C.P.A.

Like many other great and good things which have come to light, the School of Commerce, Accounts, and Finance was born of necessity. Prior to the founding of this School, the practicing accountants of the City of New York, and probably of all the United States, felt most keenly that so far as concerned the training of the future generation in the practice of accounting, there was no school other than the School of Hard Knocks and Experience. The literature on accountancy was not very extensive, and much of it would not apply to the needs of this country. The accountants did not often come together, so that there was seldom an interchanging of professional ideas and thoughts. The accountant knew little of finances, little of commercial law, not any too much of economics, and so far as his knowledge of accountancy was concerned, it was limited to his own practice.

The profession might have continued for another decade in its modest field of usefulness, were it not for the keen insight of some of the more thoughtful men; they were able to foresee that the science of accountancy could not be overestimated as to its importance, and that to rise to the fullness of usefulness, accountancy should stand upon as good a foundation as did other professions. I must here refer to the passing of the Certified Public Accountants' Law. In 1897, through the efforts of certain accountants, among whom I recall Francis Gottsberger, Frank Broaker, Charles W. Haskins, Rodney S. Dennis, John Hourigan, E. W. Sells, H. R. M. Cook, and others, the Legislature of the State of New York passed the C. P. A. Law. Shortly after, in the spring of 1897, the New York State Society of Certified Public Accountants was incorporated. It did not take many meetings before the all-important question—"Education"—came to the front. It was at once recognized that there could be no worthy profession if there was no seat of learning. Moreover, the first State Board of Examiners, which consisted of Charles W. Haskins, Frank Broaker, and Charles E. Sprague, must have anxiously considered the total absence of a school which would be able to graduate successful candidates for the C. P. A. certificate. It matters little whether the fear of no successful C. P. A. candidates or the desire to educate properly the rising generation was the direct cause of the founding of this School; the fact remains that at the November, 1899, meeting of the New York State Society of Certified Public Accountants, Mr. Henry R. M. Cook introduced a resolution requesting the President to confer with the Trustees of the University of the State of New York for the purpose of arranging for the establishment of a class for a technical course of study in the science of accounts, finance, and economy, business practice, commercial law, and so forth, and, moreover, the President was invited to co-operate with kindred societies in this State for the purpose of successfully carrying out this resolution. Mr. Haskins, who was then President of the New York State Society of Certified Public Accountants, on December 11, 1899, wrote to Chancellor Henry M. MacCracken requesting a conference with the object of effecting an agreement for the establishment of a technical course of study in the science of accounts, whereby to extend to the large and important body of accountants, and those desiring to become such accountants, an opportunity to acquire the necessary technical education. Mr. Haskins, in his letter, goes on to say:

"The grave and urgent necessity for a carefully-educated body of public accountants has been demonstrated with much force in recent years, and this necessity is particularly emphasized at this time in view of the fast-increasing number of public and semi-public corporations in which vast amounts of individual capital are invested.

"The ranks of these certified public accountants have not been materially augmented during the past two years, because intending applicants for the degree have found it difficult to obtain the required technical education before entering for examination. A respectable number of accountants have, indeed, gained experience in the employ of certain accounting firms, and have acquired the necessary technical learning by special reading at night. But these, as may be readily understood, are exceptional cases, busy expert accountants finding it very difficult to eke out time and opportunity for the instruction of their younger brethren.

"The establishment of the profession of accountancy upon an educational foundation is manifestly its only safeguard, and the one proper educational foundation would seem to lie in a university connection, such a connection as the Society I have the honor to represent may, we trust, be enabled to effect with your venerable institution.

"We recall with regret the attempts that have heretofore been made to establish independent schools of accounting. We believe that the failure of these attempts has been due to the absence of this very university foundation which we have the honor to suggest to you."

You will note that the letter which I have just read refers to the fact that previous attempts had been made to establish some such school. On one occasion the Regents of the State of New York had granted a provisional charter to a school of accounts, but after being in existence for less than one year the school surrendered its charter.

Following this letter to Chancellor MacCracken, Mr. Haskins had an interview with the Chancellor, and Mr. Haskins was encouraged to arrange a conference at his house, at which conference, in addition to Chancellor MacCracken, were present the members of a Committee from the New York State Society;

this Committee consisted of Charles W. Haskins, President; H. R. M. Cook, Chairman; J. R. Loomis, O. A. Kittredge, and myself. I think Mr. Sells was also present. Another conference was also held at Mr. Haskins' house, and finally we were requested to prepare a course of study. This was done, and at a meeting of the Committee, held at the office of Mr. James G. Cannon, this course of study was submitted to him as representing New York University.

Following this, in 1900, the School of Commerce, Accounts, and Finance was formally opened, about fifty or sixty students enrolling during the first year. The students of this School were permitted to enter certain classes of the Law School, and, other than the teachers of those Law School classes, there were but six teachers of accounting, one teacher of economics, and one other instructor. I know that, judging from my own class, the accounting knowledge of the students was so ungraded, the knowledge of the teacher and his ability to teach was so uncertain, and the confidence of the scholars, who were continually asking for instruction in higher accountancy, was so wanting, that nothing but the persistent efforts, personal encouragement, and glorious example of Charles W. Haskins kept the School from following the footpaths of those schools which had gone before. As I look upon this scene and upon the inexperience of the early teachers, the absolute absence of guiding precedents, the want of literature, the eagerness of all those students of more than average intellect for instruction in accounting, it is not at all surprising that the older and unschooled accountants of today fear to undertake the duties of a teacher in this School, but leave this task mostly for the men who have been graduated from the School.

While acknowledging the debt which we owe to members of the profession, some of whom I have already mentioned, our indebtedness to Mr. Haskins in the labor of founding the School of Commerce, Accounts, and Finance is not measurable.

As to his conception of the profession, I quote from Mr. Haskins' lecture of Ocotber 2, 1900, wherein he says:

"The ideal conception by the profession itself of its true mission, a conception from within and not dependent upon extraneous exigencies, places accountancy far outside the pale of ordinary callings and sets it upon a platform of its own as a learned profession, self-impelled to culture, to moral enlargement, and to scientific attainment; and lays a basis of confidence for every business enterprise that in professional accountancy there is a self-centered soul of economic truth."

In one of the catalogues of the New York University we see, under the heading of History and Statutes, that New York University owes its foundation and its progress until this date to two classes of citizens: first, the public-spirited merchants, bankers, and professional men, who have given labor and money to promote liberal learning in the metropolis upon the higher academic models. To this class could no one be better accredited than Charles Waldo Haskins.

PRESENTATION OF TABLET

By H. M. James, Class of 1910

Ten years ago Charles Waldo Haskins, with other accountants and prominent men of this city, decided that there should be opportunity for higher commercial education offered to the young people of this country. These men recognized that not only was a theoretical training valuable in business, but that a practical education could be given in a university; that a long apprenticeship at actual work would not necessarily best fit the young man for his life occupation; that many of the mistakes of our "practical" business men had come from the very lack of scientific training. To this end the School of Commerce, Accounts, and Finance was created. And one of the foremost of its creators was the man who became its first Dean.

There was more than this desire to extend educational privileges, in Mr. Haskins' accomplishment. Had it not been for his indefatigable energy, his constant endeavor, and his loving thought, the School would not stand where it does today. Now its graduates are scattered over the world in nearly every variety of profession and of business occupation. The need for its training is undoubtedly felt by young men, and the advantages are widely recognized by employers. To the latter, the fact that a prospective employee is a graduate of the School does not mean what college training once meant to the employer. The degree or certificate from the School means a practical and thorough training in business which, while it does not do away with the need for actual experience, does mean that the young man so trained need not start at sweeping out the office.

The Class of 1910 entered the School in the fall of 1907, nearly 300 strong. We soon learned that the establishment and growth of the School had been due, in large measure, to the efforts and the foresight of one man. Mr. Haskins' name was frequently mentioned. Personally, I was very fortunate early in my school career in meeting a number of graduates, some of whom had known Mr. Haskins, and they told me of him. Many of our lecturers referred to him and his work.

Therefore, as we were about to close our university career, we thought that we could not leave with our Alma Mater a more suitable token of our sincere gratitude for the knowledge gained within her walls than a tablet in memory of her first Dean, the late Charles Waldo Haskins. At first, we planned that it should be given merely by the Class of 1910. But members of the Alumni and friends of Mr. Haskins were so anxious to co-operate with us that finally we consented to let all who would, help us to make this tablet worthy of the man in whose memory it is given.

Much as we owe to the past and present members of the Faculty, and to our present Dean, we recognize the obligation we owe to the first Dean. In order, to a very small extent, to pay our respect and to do honor to his memory; and to give some token of our gratitude, we are gathered here tonight. Therefore, on behalf of the graduates and of the students, and especially on behalf of my own Class of 1910, I present through you, Dean Johnson, to the School, this memorial. And I ask that it be hung in the Commerce Halls: that all returning graduates, that all visitors, that all future students may understand our gratitude, and help us to give honor where honor is due, to the first Dean, Charles Waldo Haskins.

HASKINS' MEMORIAL

By Joseph French Johnson, D.C.S., LL.D.

Members of the Class of 1910, Alumni of the School of Commerce, and friends of Charles Waldo Haskins:

This is an occasion of personal and professional interest to me, for I had the privilege of knowing Mr. Haskins as a teacher and as a dean most intimately. For the two years preceding his death I was in daily touch with him, and I became deeply attached to him as a friend, and thoroughly trustful in his ability and unselfishness as an educational leader. He was one of the most modest and unassuming men I ever knew. If he could speak to us out of the Great Silence, I know he would say: "Waste no time and spend no money in honor of me. Give your thought always to the present and the future." We, nevertheless—and I speak for the Faculty of the School of Commerce, Accounts, and Finance—believe that this beautiful tablet is destined to do more than perpetuate a personal memory. As the memorial of a business man who in middle life successfully devoted himself to the realization of a new ideal in education, this tablet will be treasured not merely because it preserves in enduring bronze the features of Charles

Waldo Haskins, but also because it symbolizes the immortality of his achievement, and will, we are sure, prove an inspiration to thousands of young men and young women in future years. Therefore, as Dean of the Faculty of the School of Commerce, Accounts, and Finance, and with the due authority from the Council of New York University, I announce to you, Mr. James, representing the Class of 1910, and to all the other donors, that this gift is most gratefully accepted and will be given appropriate setting in the halls of the School of Commerce, Accounts, and Finance.

www.ingramcontent.com/pod-product-compliance
Lightning Source LLC
Chambersburg PA
CBHW021147090426
42740CB00008B/991